HELPFUL

A Guide to Life, Careers, and the Art of Networking

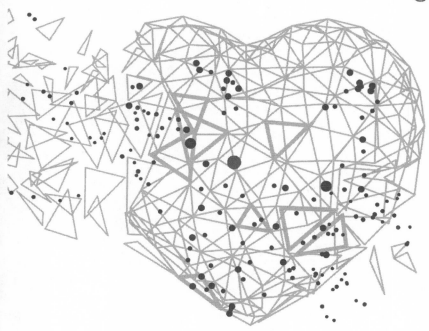

HEATHER HOLLICK

HELPFUL

A Guide to Life, Careers and the Art of Networking

HEATHER HOLLICK

Orinda Vista Press
Traverse City, Michigan

ISBN 978-1-7329459-0-6 (Hardcover)
ISBN 978-1-7329459-1-3 (Paperback)
ISBN 978-1-7329459-2-0 (eBook)

Library of Congress Control Number: 2018914510

Published by Orinda Vista Press, www.orindavista.com
Quantity Sales: Special discounts are available on quantity purchases. For details contact sales@orindavista.com

Printed in the United States of America

Editing by Ashleigh Imus.
Illustrations by Lorraine Yow.
Cover design by Cathi Stevenson at BookCoverExpress.com.
Layout and interior design by Gwen Gades at beapurplepenguin.com.

For my fellow seekers...

Contents

You are not an isolated entity, but a unique, irreplaceable part of the cosmos. Don't forget this. You are an essential piece of the puzzle of humanity. Each of us is a part of a vast, intricate, and perfectly ordered human community. But where do you fit into this web of humanity? To whom are you beholden?

Look for and come to understand your connections to other people. We properly locate ourselves within the cosmic scheme by recognizing our natural relations to one another and thereby identifying our duties. Our duties naturally emerge from such fundamental relations as our families, neighborhoods, workplaces, our state or nation. Make it your regular habit to consider your roles — parent, child, neighbor, citizen, leader — and the natural duties that arise from them. Once you know who you are and to whom you are linked, you will know what to do.

Epictetus, c. 55 – 135 AD

From The Art of Living, A New Interpretation by Sharon Lebell[1]

Preface

This is a book about professional networking. It is also a book about livelihoods, about some of the key differences between introverts and extraverts, and how to make a difference in the world. At its core it's a how-to manual for building your own tribe in a world where the people with whom we work—and the people with whom we *should be working*—are spread around the globe. In such a fast-moving, ever-changing environment, not networking is not an option.

This book grew out of my gradual awakening to the anemic nature of traditional networking. I had long known that I wasn't very good at networking, but I slowly came to the realization that most other people weren't very good at it, either. Compounding the issue was my eventual realization that the cultural norms surrounding networking were shallow and often backwards. I found most "networking" events to be utterly fruitless. For the life of me I couldn't figure out how screaming at someone in a noisy bar qualified as networking. I couldn't shake the nagging sense that something was missing. There had to be more to networking than that.

Our culture is laced with the conventional wisdom that networking is important. I had no reason to doubt this conventional wisdom, but what I was observing and experiencing didn't seem like networking to me. What I saw looked superficial. What I experienced felt awkward and unproductive.

So, I set out on a mission to develop an understanding of networking—an understanding that would work not only for me but also in our modern economy. As an amateur psychologist and an emerging coach, I also felt it was important to find an approach to networking that resonated across a range of personalities, preferences, and styles. I questioned everything and took nothing for granted. I wove together my knowledge of business and economics with my understanding of personality and the human mind to articulate an approach to networking that finally made sense to me. The results of my explorations are the ideas, principles, and techniques laid out in the pages ahead.

I hope that you find this approach to networking as compelling as I do. My wish is that you learn how to network effectively much earlier in your career than I did. It is critical to your success in your job, in your career, and in life.

Source Material

The research for this book comes through a lifetime of study, immersion, and intense observation. I draw upon a broad range of experiences encompassing my work as a seasoned leader, teacher, coach, and change-agent across multiple disciplines—including IT, HR, consulting, and volunteer organizations; across industries—such as health insurance, high tech, consulting, the public sector, and volunteer organizations; and spanning such companies as Cisco Systems, United Healthcare, Research in Motion, and the Pensions Department of the British Government.

I've led—and been led by—some amazing people. I've had the privilege to lead organizations as large as 250 people and manage a portfolio of projects with combined budgets in excess of $100 million. I have successfully overseen the delivery of numerous highly complex projects with a broad range of constituents and stakeholders. The pinnacle of all projects involved leading the update of 162,000 desktop and laptop computers from Windows 2000 to Windows XP.[2] Anyone who has tried to upgrade a *single* computer from one version of an operating system to the next can appreciate the complexity of multiplying this by 162,000. After a rough start prior to my arrival, the upgrades proceeded over the course of nine months with minimal disruption.

Learning is my first love. In addition to reading widely on various topics, I have a master's degree in applied mathematics from Purdue University and an MBA from the University of California at Berkeley. I have also delighted in graduate-level courses in computer science, philosophy, psychology, and counseling. The logical precision of my mathematical training combined with the global perspective afforded by an MBA from a top-tier university fit perfectly with my passion for well-defined solutions that work across many contexts.

My nomadic lifestyle also forced me to learn about networking. While I have occasionally envied people who are grounded in a single place, my life has brought me across Canada, the United States, and the United Kingdom. I have lived and worked in Southern Ontario, Canada, England, the American Midwest, the American Southwest, northern California, the Northeast, the mid-Atlantic South, and now, once again, in the Great Lakes Region. Each place was a crucible of learning, offering its own culture and lessons in how people and teams best work together.

My interests range from philosophy, epistemology, and psychology, to the grandeur and majesty of nature. I can engage deeply in topics as varied as team culture, economics, politics, logistics, complex systems, technology, movie and television production, and wine and craft cocktails. You are as likely to catch me reading a book on indigenous populations as on Steph Curry and the Golden State Warriors. Not surprisingly, most of these interests find their way into the ideas and techniques you'll discover in the following pages.

In 2007, as I moved away from the corporate world and pivoted to a career in leadership development and coaching, I began to share my approach to networking through talks, workshops, and webinars. My audiences—who, like me, wanted more from their lives and careers—became part of a virtuous feedback loop. Each presentation was a living laboratory that brought a little more insight and clarity.

Very quickly an amazing thing started to happen. People talked of light bulbs going off in their heads as I reframed their thinking on professional relationships. They breathed a sigh of relief as I set them free to be themselves. They incorporated my techniques to improve their networking both inside and outside of their organizations.

Mostly, they encouraged me to tell more people. And so, after more than ten years of development, dozens of talks and presentations, and hundreds of hours of one-on-one coaching, here we are: a book about networking, careers, team dynamics, professional relationships, and, in many ways, life.

The Road Ahead

The journey that we are about to undertake comprises four distinct segments. In *Part I — Preparation,* I make the case for networking and tell how it grew out of my life experience and my ineptitude at savvy networking. I explore several contrasts along the spectrum of introversion and extraversion. Understanding your preferences along this spectrum, as well as learning to recognize the preferences of others, is crucial to all of the work that follows. Throughout the book I encourage you to develop an approach to networking that melds deeply with your style and the personality preferences that shape who you are.

In *Part II — The Networking Mindset,* I define how to *think* about networking. In Chapter 6, we'll explore the essence of a network. Then, in Chapter 7, we'll build on this notion and define networking as an active and invigorating way of engaging with the world. With a pragmatic definition of networking, we'll then explore how to quickly move through the banalities of small-talk to engage deeply in a way that helps to build mutually beneficial relationships.

In *Part III — Networking in Action,* we take our newfound ideas and put them into practice across scenarios ranging from one-on-one meetings to conferences and large events. We also explore how to leverage the power of LinkedIn, and other social media, to build and maintain your network.

Finally, in *Part IV — Networking at Work,* I show how our basic mindset of networking can work within organizations to become an invaluable career tool and a transformational cultural norm. In our modern, complex world you simply must have a robust network if you want to have any kind of career success. I will argue that, beyond individual success, if a critical mass of individuals within an organization embrace the networking mindset, they will create a culture of collaboration that most companies only dream about.

Move the World

Your network is a powerful tool that you begin creating early in your career and carry with you for the rest of your life. It stays with you from job to job and career to career. It is entirely your own creation, and no one can take it away from you. If you do it well, you can build a network that becomes your tribe — *the people to whom you are loyal and who, you trust, are loyal to you.*

My goal is to not only help you understand how to build and maintain a network but also to enable you to leverage that network for all its power. Archimedes, often considered the father of physics, understood the power of leverage. He said, "Give me a lever and a place to stand and I will move the world." The place to stand is where you are standing now, wherever you happen to be in your career and in your life. The lever is your network, the interconnected web of relationships that you build and maintain over the course of your career.

You are part of something larger than yourself. You are a member of a family, a community, a country, an economy. You are part of the body politic. And you are part of the human race. Each of those realms offers an obligation and an opportunity for you to make your mark. Join me in embracing this approach to networking. As each of us builds our individual networks, we become ever more interconnected. The result will be a vast human network with enough leverage and force to move the world many times over.

I have a dream of making the world a better place to work. Join me in embracing the world with a spirit of helpfulness. Your career — and our world — depends on it.

To our success...

Part I
Preparation For Our Journey

Chapter 1

First Principles

*Principles could be seen as the soil that
derive from the bedrock of values.*

George Monbiot[3]

How we see the world derives from what we are capable of seeing. While that may sound like a tautology, what I mean is that in most cases, we can only see what we are looking for. Over the years we develop a base of principles, values, and beliefs that shape what we see and how we comprehend the world. These principles and beliefs become a lens through which we experience the world.

As we begin our journey into networking, I owe it to you to first illuminate where I'm coming from. I have two principles that underlie everything we are going to talk about. Upon these "first principles" I will lay a mindset that frames our understanding of networking. Then, with a fresh mindset, I will put forth practical and sensible tools and techniques that you can use to become master networkers.

Everything in this book builds on these fundamental principles. If you find they resonate with your values, then I invite you to read on. If you see the world through a lens like mine, then what I have to offer will make tremendous sense, and you will find much here to enhance your life and bolster your career.

1. We Are All Interconnected

It is often said that humans are social creatures. Very true. But we are much more than merely social. Humans are a thoroughly interconnected species. This deep interconnectedness has enabled a phenomenal degree of interdependence. As we move through our lives, we weave in and out of a web of dependencies on myriad levels: physical, emotional, social, economic, and political.

- **Physical:** Evidence indicates the existence of mirror neurons in our brains that fire when we observe behaviors in others. Our brains behave as if we were the ones acting.[4]

- **Emotional:** We are interconnected through our empathic capacity to understand and share the feelings of others.[*]

- **Social:** Aristotle was the first to declare that humans are social animals.[†] Over the millennia since his keen insight, we have come to explore and understand the true power of this interconnectedness. In his recent book, *The Secret of Our Success,* Joseph Henrich shows that our collective intelligence, our ability to learn from one another, and our cumulative history have enabled us to produce sophisticated languages, complex institutions, and amazing technologies. Alone, we stand naked against the elements. Together, the human race has come to dominate the globe more than any other species has.[5]

- **Economic:** The food we eat, every object we touch, every product we buy, every public service we use has come to us through a vast network of interconnected people. Despite what we often hear in the public and political spheres, there is no such thing as a "self-made" person. We are interconnected and interdependent.

---

* I readily admit that not everyone has the capacity for empathy. Some estimate that as many as 4% of the population lack it completely. See *The Sociopath Next Door* by Martha Stout, Ph.D., for a fascinating exploration of sociopathy and its implications.

† "Man is by nature a social animal; an individual who is unsocial naturally and not accidentally is either beneath our notice or more than human. Society is something that precedes the individual. Anyone who either cannot lead the common life or is so self-sufficient as not to need to, and therefore does not partake of society, is either a beast or a god." Aristotle, *Politics.*

- **Political:** In democratic societies, we individually decide how we want to be led and collectively exercise our democratic privileges to elect the people who lead us.

2. People Want to Be Helpful

The second principle that guides us on this journey is that people want to be helpful. They really do! Human beings are an incredibly altruistic species. I cannot possibly explain it any better than George Monbiot does in his insightful and hopeful book, *Out of the Wreckage: A New Politics for an Age of Crisis*:

> *By the age of fourteen months, children begin to help each other, attempting to hand over objects another child cannot reach. By the time they are two, they start sharing some of the things they value. By the age of three, they start to protest against other people's violations of moral norms.*
>
> *We are also, among mammals (with the possible exception of the naked mole rat), the supreme cooperators. We evolved in the African savannahs: a world of fangs and claws and horns and tusks. We survived despite being weaker and slower than both our potential predators and most of our prey. We did so through developing, to an extraordinary degree, a capacity for mutual aid. As it was essential to our survival, this urge to cooperate was hard-wired into our brains through natural selection. It has not been lost.[6]*

Building mutually beneficial relationships that leverage the interconnectedness of our being and the intersection of our talents, knowledge, and networks is what brings success and will ultimately move humanity forward.

Chapter 2

An Introvert's Journey

It ain't what you don't know that gets you into trouble.
It's what you know for sure that just ain't so.

Unknown

We have an odd relationship with the concept of networking. We all seem to know it's important, but few of us seem to know how to do it well. I see many people going through the motions, but few give much thought to what they are doing. While there's no shortage of meet-ups and networking events, the return on our investment of time and energy in those events is disappointing. Many of us are at a loss when it comes to building powerful, professional relationships.

Our relationship with networking is not unlike our cultural relationship with dancing. Dancing is a joyous, often visceral activity. However, it is assumed that everyone *can* dance and that everyone enjoys doing so. That is far from the case.

Think back to the last time you were at an event that featured dancing—perhaps a recent wedding. Take your mind back to that dance floor and remember what you saw there.

My guess is that you saw a wide variety of skill and movement:

- There were, no doubt, a few people who were exceptionally good dancers. Their bodies were at one with the music, moving with the rhythm, naturals on the dance floor. These people were in their element and were enjoying themselves.

- There were a fair number of people—perhaps the majority—who were just okay dancers. They bobbed and wove in predictable, repeatable patterns. Occasionally they lost the beat, paused, and reset. It's not clear if they were enjoying themselves, but they had succumbed to social pressures and made themselves get out on the floor just the same.

- There were a small number of people who were simply bad dancers. They flailed around the dance floor as if they had just been stung by a hive of bees. They knew they weren't very good at dancing and, proudly, didn't seem to care.

- Finally, there were the wallflowers — the people who knew they weren't very good dancers and made the conscious choice to keep off the floor. Some were shy, just waiting to be asked. Others were honest enough to know that they would not enjoy themselves in any way if they so much as set foot on the dance floor.

I have long considered myself a proud member of the Wallflower Club when it comes to dancing. No apologies. No shame. So my intention is in no way to cast aspersions on people's dancing skills — far from it. Dancing is a physical manifestation of our love of music and our joy at being alive. Let your body move. However, dancing is an apt metaphor for our modern approach to networking. And while our individual talents for dancing have little impact on our careers, networking matters deeply to our individual success and, as we shall see, the success of our teams and organizations.

To see some of the parallels between dancing and networking, consider the dancers in the first group, the extraordinary dancers. We often marvel at their talents without giving much thought to how they got to be so good. The truth is, they weren't born that way. They might have been blessed with some natural rhythm and a desire to move, but they were not born good dancers. Whether they took formal dancing lessons, studied YouTube videos in the privacy of their living rooms,[7] or simply practiced their hearts out, they deliberately set out to be good. They invested the time and the effort necessary to learn how to become great dancers.

The world of networking and professional relationships has much the same categories of people. In general, networking skills are all over the map. Interpersonal abilities range from seemingly invisible wallflowers and ineffective flailing to sublime connectors who seem to know everyone and are always willing to share what they know or make an introduction. And, like dancing, the master networkers were not born that way. The best networkers invested the time and the effort to learn how to connect with people, how to listen, and how to be helpful. Along the way, they built a web of professional relationships that nourishes their careers, extends its reach with each new connection, and increases in power with each passing day.

I started on the networking dance floor as a wallflower—with occasional forays into ineffective flailing. Over the course of too many years, I slowly awoke to the rich world of professional relationships that was missing from my career and my life. Determined to be a better networker, I was relieved to discover that my shortcomings were neither genetically determined nor culturally preordained. Instead, while I had much to learn about social skills, the real problem was that the conventional wisdom on networking was upside down and backwards. I am nowhere near a sublime connector yet, but I have found a perspective and approach for networking that makes it easy and natural.

My Story

In many ways, I am an unlikely candidate to be teaching about professional networking. Although I have come to embrace the intentional act of networking as an essential skill for success in the twenty-first century, there was a time when the mere thought of talking about myself—and especially small talk—practically paralyzed me. I accepted my ineptness at networking as my fate. You play the hand you're dealt, I thought. Much later in life, I figured out that the hand you are dealt isn't nearly as important as the game in which you choose to play it. I learned to deal myself into a different game, one for which the hand I was dealt is much better suited.

I did not grow up with a strong need for social skills. My childhood home was rural, along a river in Southern Ontario, Canada. My combined elementary and middle school was small: six classrooms spanning eight grades serving fewer than 200 students. Extracurricular and after-school activities were rare. I spent more time playing in the nearby woods and along the river than I ever did interacting with other people.

Nor were social skills among the many gifts my parents passed on to me. My folks were simple, hard-working people. During my youth my mom labored through shift work as a nursing assistant. My dad was a bricklayer and made his living in the brutal outdoor world of building and construction in our often-harsh northern clime. The closest my parents ever came to offering career advice was when my dad suggested that I read Dale Carnegie's book *How to Win Friends and Influence People.**

Most important, I accepted my fate as a sub-par networker because I am an introvert. If you gave me the option to stay home with a good book versus going out with a group of people... well... I'd take the deal—even if it meant being stuck with a *bad* book. I fell for the misconception that introverts can't be good networkers. Although I sensed that my aversion to social activity was a liability, I figured, "It is what it is." As Popeye always says, "I yam what I yam."[8]

Tired of the cold winters, which wreak havoc on a bricklayer's hands, my father took us from one extreme to the other. The summer after my sophomore year in high school, he sold our country home in the cool climates of Southern Ontario, Canada and moved our family to the desert heat of Lake Havasu City, Arizona. For my introduction to America, I found myself an early settler in a planned and promoted city in the middle of the Mojave Desert.[9]

The disruption caused by moving from a bucolic life along a quiet river in Canada to an enterprising outpost in the desert Southwest shaped my understanding of America. It started a nomadic adventure that continues to this day. I have had the good fortune to live in

---

* Looking back, I realize now that my father was on to something. I wish I had listened to him.

numerous cities and communities in eight states across the US as well as a brief return to work in Canada and a two-year stint in the UK.

Despite my lack of networking skills, I did okay for the first half of my career. I completed college in Indiana and started my twenties as a high-school math teacher in a nearby town. I left high-school teaching after two years and wrapped up the decade working on a couple of graduate degrees, including a master's degree in applied mathematics, which I completed, and a master's in philosophy, which I did not. As I approached my thirtieth birthday I found myself in Denver, Colorado, studying philosophy and counseling. While Colorado embodies a majestic corner of the world, it was rapidly becoming clear to me that the life of a perpetual student left much to be desired, not the least of which was health care. A friend had just started in an entry-level position at an insurance company and paved the way for an interview. To my relief, they hired me.

My initial foray into the corporate world went deceptively well. My ability to contribute was almost instantly recognized and appreciated. I moved up quickly. Within a year I was offered a relocation to Albuquerque, and three years later I transferred to San Francisco. My newfound corporate career seemed to be on the fast track.

I arrived in San Francisco in the mid 1990s. The technology revolution was in full swing and the spirit of the original 49ers filled the air[10] — only this time we weren't searching for gold. We were inventing the future. I moved on from the insurance company in due time and joined the throngs of tech-heads who were changing jobs and companies every couple of years. I eventually landed at Cisco Systems on the eve of Y2K. It was a booming company at the leading edge of the technology revolution.

Unfortunately, the tech revolution was overheating and the dot-com bubble[11] was about to burst. Around the same time, it was becoming clear that my career had hit the doldrums as well. Despite good performance reviews and a great boss, advancement eluded me. All I ever seemed to get for doing good work was more of the same: new assignments that looked much like the old assignments. I felt invisible...and stuck.

Naturally, I did what any mid-career, forty-something professional in a rut would do: I decided to go back to school. I was accepted into the Evening MBA program at UC Berkeley and dedicated myself to my studies. My intuitive and introverted mind was in heaven as I immersed myself in the expansive worlds of macroeconomics, business and public policy, and organizational behavior. Business school was an exciting peek behind the curtain at how the business world really worked.

Unbeknownst to me at the time, most people pursue MBA degrees for three reasons: the content of the courses, the credibility of the institution, and the network. While I lapped up the course material, and was humbled to have been admitted to the hallowed halls of such a credible institution, I was naïve to the power of the network I had so innocently joined. My classmates, however, quickly brought me up to speed. People couldn't stop talking about how excited they were to be a part of the Berkeley Alumni Network.

As the reality of their words sunk in, it was as if a thousand dormant desert flowers had just been splashed with a spring rain. Eureka! Being part of a network was the missing ingredient in my career. While my preference for introversion and, more important, my lack of social skills had caught up with me, fate had smiled on me once again. The answer was right in front of me: networking was the key ingredient missing from my career.

It didn't take long to figure out that being back in school offered a very brief window to learn and master networking—the essential skill I knew I lacked. I committed myself to learn networking with the same gusto that I was learning economics. I was soon a regular at every class mixer, bar-of-the-week, pub-of-the-month, and Friday afternoon social I could find.

At first it was fun. The energy—not to mention some of the refreshments—was intoxicating. However, I still had this nagging sense that something was missing. Was this it? For the life of me I couldn't figure out how screaming to be heard in a noisy bar qualified as networking. It was all but impossible to have a meaningful conversation in a room where the combined conversations were so loud that I couldn't even hear myself think. At best, we were enjoying the beer, exchanging pleasantries, and performing the gratuitous exchange of business cards. There had to be more to networking than that.

I retreated and regrouped. Despite my misgivings about some of the activities billed as "networking events," I knew intuitively that networking was the missing key to career success. For years I had been a wallflower, fading into the background and hoping that my good work would speak for itself, all the while ignoring the importance of networking and building relationships. When I finally stepped onto the dance floor, I was ill prepared. I found myself flailing to a beat that I either could not hear or did not understand.

Undeterred, I continued to participate, watch, and learn. I had gone into this knowing I wasn't very good at networking. It would take me another five years before it would finally dawn on me that other people weren't that good at it, either.

This was a huge revelation. Most networkers looked like the mediocre dancers on the dance floor: they missed steps, they missed beats, and they didn't seem to care. Granted, they had the social courage to get themselves out on the dance floor in the first place, but very few of them appeared to know what they were doing.

And yet, there were those few shining stars — the master networkers who could work a room with grace and aplomb. They were magnets, and hubs, and amplifiers. They made introductions and they got introduced. They moved effortlessly through a room.

As I learned about — and from — these master networkers, I realized that networking skills were a subset of social skills. And I knew that there was nothing magic about social skills. They are neither genetic nor innate. Social skills are learned. Most of us, if we're lucky, are blessed with caring adults in our lives who instill social skills in us from an early age. The master networkers I was seeing had simply had the good fortune to learn networking skills earlier in their career.

I was relieved to conclude that good networking was not natural; it was learned. And if there was one thing I was good at, it was learning. I set off in search of an answer to the simple question, "What is networking?"

I mean, really, what *IS* networking? I was confident I knew what it wasn't: standing in noisy bars screaming to be heard. But it would take a bit of a journey to figure out what networking was—and more important, what networking was *for me.*

The rest of this book is a travelogue of sorts. I share my stories and insights from my journey to discover networking, in the hope that you will wake to the power of networking much earlier in your career than I did. If enough of us start embracing the world with this new mindset, we just might make a dent in the universe. At the very least, we'll make the world a better place to work.

Chapter 3

Know Thyself

Be yourself. Everyone else is already taken.

Unknown[12]

As we begin our journey into the world of networking, the first step is a little self-exploration. Networking is a deeply personal endeavor. As such, before we can learn how to build mutually beneficial relationships, we need to get a clearer sense of our personal style, how we prefer to communicate, and *where* we think. In so doing, I hope that you will gain a better understanding not only of yourself but also the art of identifying—and adapting to—the styles and preferences of others.

This is not a book specifically *for* introverts. While I am confident that most introverts will find it invaluable, it will be equally valuable to people with a preference for extraversion. I contrast introverts and extraverts not to appeal to any particular preference but to highlight that people respond to other people in different ways. As a result, different people should network differently. One of the biggest social mistakes we make is to assume that other people think and communicate the same way we do. Nowhere is this more pronounced than along the introvert-extravert spectrum. I cringe every time I see an article about networking that does not factor in the fundamental differences between introverts and extraverts, as if the same four bullet points on "how to network" apply to everyone universally.

It is impossible to overstate how important it is for you to find your own approach to networking. In my experience, the networking styles most effective for introverts are markedly different from those typically embraced by extraverts. We are both right. Building and maintaining professional relationships that are mutually beneficial is a lifelong journey. My intention is that you will be able to find a style within these pages that's right for you.

A Note on Terms

I am often asked about my choice to spell the word as "extravert" rather than "extrovert." While the differences might be subtle, "extravert" and "extrovert" are two different words. In general usage, an "extrovert" refers to a gregarious and unreserved person *(Merriam-Webster).* The word "extravert"—as originally coined by Carl Jung—refers to "someone whose attention and interests are directed wholly or predominantly toward what is outside the self" *(Merriam-Webster Unabridged).* This makes sense, given that in Latin, "extra" means outside and "vertere" means to turn. So, an "extravert" turns outward.

I use "extravert" because the term, used extensively in the psychology literature, more closely describes the personality dimensions that are helpful for understanding how to build and maintain relationships with people. When relating to people, it is important to know whether a person's attention is focused inward or outward. Whether they are gregarious or unreserved is an entirely different matter, and I have met both introverts and extraverts who display these characteristics. Hence, I will use the terms introvert and extravert for the opposite ends of this highly relevant Myers-Briggs spectrum. For further exploration of the etymology and use of both words, see the brilliant entry "Extrovert or extravert?" on *The Grammarphobia Blog.*[13]

Myths of Extraversion

Some of the biggest challenges in building and maintaining relationships emerge in the gaps and misunderstandings between introverts and extraverts. There's a popular myth, particularly in US culture, that extraverts are better networkers than introverts. Or perhaps you've seen the unfortunate corollary to this myth, aimed specifically at the shy and/or introverted, naively counseling them simply to be more extraverted to be a better networker.

I count at least two implicit—and deeply flawed—assumptions in these simplistic and misguided assertions. First, these myths assume that what we see extraverts doing in social situations is, in fact, networking. I have no doubt that extraverts often *think* they are better networkers. I also have no doubt that many extraverts believe the way they are interacting with others constitutes networking. Too often they are the ones who look like the inept dancer on the dance floor flailing and floundering, always a half-beat out of sync with the music.

To be fair, people with a preference for extraversion start from a good place in the networking arena. Extraverts have a natural propensity to be congenial and talkative. They connect easily with other people and often have a broad base of acquaintances. Further, many extraverts are continuously on the lookout for new people and are generous about making introductions. However, when it comes to building mutually beneficial relationships, these behaviors are just table stakes. In and of themselves, they are not necessarily networking.

Networking skills are simply a subset of social skills, and social skills are learned—they are not natural to anyone. Where you fall on the introvert-extravert spectrum is separate and independent of your proficiency as a networker. Some extraverts have learned networking skills; many have not. Same for introverts. Both introverts and extraverts can learn networking skills equally well, although each will manifest those skills quite differently.

The second assumption implicit in the assertion that better networking simply requires one to be more extraverted is that there is only *one way* to network: the way that we see most extraverts networking. Reality is much more nuanced—and freeing—than that. There are an infinite variety of ways to network—as infinite as the combination of people, personality types, and preferences. The key is to find an approach that works for you and a style that leverages your strengths and preferences.

What's the Difference?

In the last few years a cornucopia of well-written books and articles have articulated and differentiated the styles and preferences of introverts and extraverts. Susan Cain's work appears to have been the tipping point. Her book *Quiet: The Power of Introverts in a World That Can't Stop Talking*[14] was amplified by her very popular TED Talk.[15] With her tireless efforts to raise awareness, Susan seems to have pushed aversion to introversion past a tipping point, moving it from the murky shadows of a perceived malady and into the limelight of normalcy. It seems that America has finally embraced the fact that introversion and extraversion simply reflect different preferences and styles for interacting with the world, while having no bearing on intelligence, talent, potential, ambition, ability to contribute, or any other ill-conceived category that the world uses to measure success.

We can't begin to cover all the differences between introverts and extraverts, so we'll dig into a few that are most relevant to networking and interacting with others. First, let me be clear by what I *don't* mean by introvert and extravert.

By "introvert" I do not mean someone who is shy, averse to social contact, or misanthropic. Shyness is different from introversion. Shyness encompasses a fear of social disapproval and humiliation. While there is a slight correlation between shyness and introversion, shyness afflicts both introverts and extraverts. For both camps, shyness and social anxiety can often be overcome by determination and learning key social skills.[16]

I used to be shy. Then I taught myself the social skills that help me to effectively interact with people. I started by focusing on building a professional network and have been delighted to discover that my newfound social skills enhance all my relationships, not just the professional ones. I am no longer afraid of being rejected. My shyness has ebbed. I will, however, always have a deep preference for introversion.

Likewise, by "extravert" I do not mean a person who is bubbly, gregarious, or someone who always seeks to be the center of attention. I am thinking here of the bubbly store clerk who chirps, "How are you this fine day?" when you walk into the store. Overt gregariousness is not extraversion; it is a learned social skill. While these behaviors may correlate slightly to a preference for extraversion, they are by no means limited to extraverts, and they certainly do not define extraversion. They are learned behaviors.

So, what *do* I mean by introversion and extraversion? For our purposes, I'll look at two key elements along the introvert-extravert spectrum: what stimulates us and how our thought processes work.

What Do You Find Stimulating?

The most common aspects of the introvert-extravert spectrum usually relate to what people find energizing or stimulating. Many will suppose that the difference between introverts and extraverts centers on where you get your energy. It is commonly portrayed that extraverts get their energy from being with other people, while introverts get their energy from being alone. There is some truth to this, but it's too simple. The real differences are more nuanced. A better understanding comes when we look not at *where* we get our energy but at *what* we find stimulating—and, by contrast, by looking at what we find destimulating or draining.

Extraverted Stimulation

Drawn to the external realms of activities and people, extraverts are stimulated by the external world. They find the background conversation of a coffee shop or the buzz of a crowded bar invigorating. Conversations with other people are inherently energizing regardless of the subject. Further, most extraverts are drawn to striking up a conversation—which they find stimulating—with just about anyone they meet.

Just the sound of conversations or music in the background can be stimulating to an extravert. An extravert will often go to a coffee shop, not necessarily to speak with anyone but to soak in the energy she derives from the hum of music and multiple conversations in the background. At home, extraverts are the ones who often have the television on "just for background noise," they'll say.

Introverted Stimulation

Introverts, on the other hand, get their stimulation internally—from their inner world of thoughts, ideas, and feelings. I can speak from my own experience here: as an introvert, I am constantly thinking, processing, wondering, imagining, and connecting dots. I may have a half-dozen trains of thought running through my head *at the same time.* My quiet demeanor may betray the vibrant mental activity taking place just below the surface. Still waters run deep.

Carl Jung, who popularized the terms *introvert* and *extravert* as the central building blocks of personality, said that introverts focus on the meaning they make of the events swirling around them; extraverts plunge into the events themselves.[17] Introverts want to understand the world in order to experience it, whereas extraverts want to experience the world in order to understand it.

Earlier, I joked that, given the choice of going out with a group of people or staying home with a good book, I would opt to stay home, even if that meant staying home with a *bad* book. This makes more sense now that you understand what introverts find stimulating. Even with a bad book—perhaps especially with a bad book—my mind is active. With each painful paragraph and lame plot twist, I am rewriting the story in my head. Such activity is, in itself, stimulating. Although it can sometimes be embarrassing to admit, even a bad book can be stimulating to an introvert.

People often say that introverts prefer to be alone. This is not quite accurate. It depends on whether an introvert can also engage their mind. A day full of mindless, tedious tasks can be highly draining for an introvert. The key is for their brain to be engaged. Being alone is not necessarily stimulating. Thinking is stimulating.

There are plenty of occasions when I have been alone all day but bogged down in mundane tasks. On such days I am far from energized at the end of the day. Stimulation is independent of the presence of people. If I am doing mindless or administrative tasks, then I can be drained of energy even when working alone.

Whether or not other people are involved, introverts prefer to be in a mental place where their minds are active with ideas. At any given time, a rich world of thoughts and ideas is active in our minds. Being alone just gives us the freedom to control the thoughts. We can be equally stimulated if we are engrossed in conversation in a small group.

Large groups, on the other hand, are rarely our sweet spot. The din of a large crowd can be physically stressful, raising the cortisol[18] levels in our bloodstreams. And regardless of the group size, mindless chatter and prolonged small talk are always draining to an introvert.

Introverts find background noises distracting. I sometimes enjoy the quiet buzz of background conversations in a coffee shop, but I would never be able to do any work there that involved concentration or deep thinking.

Any noise in the background—especially conversations and human voices—comes at the expense of our ability to concentrate. If I am trying to think, I must sacrifice a portion of my mental energy just to filter out the background noises and let my mind work. The recent trend away from open office spaces[19] is an encouraging acknowledgment that introverts—about half of the population—cannot do their best work in an environment where they must expend mental energy to filter out background distractions.

Where Do You Think?

Where we get our energy is undoubtedly among the most popular framing of the differences between introverts and extraverts. However, it is not the most significant characteristic on this spectrum, especially when it comes to networking and relationships. In my professional opinion, the most profound and defining difference between introverts and extraverts is *where* we think. That is an odd phrase, "where we think." We don't often consider our thought processes as having a spatial dimension. And yet, our thoughts most certainly develop and exist in space.

Extraverted Thinking

In general—and this should come as no surprise—extraverts tend to think externally, by which I mean they need to verbalize their thoughts for them to be fully formed. Let me say that again. For an extravert, thoughts are primarily formed *as they are verbalized.* It's as if the ideas are taking shape in little thought bubbles a few inches in front of their faces.

I'm not saying that extraverts are incapable of deep thought or forming thoughts unless their mouths are moving. However, until an extravert has a chance to verbalize their thoughts, the ideas will not be fully formed, at least to their satisfaction. They need to verbalize their thoughts to fully form them. They speak to think.

I am certain that you have experienced this phenomenon. Think back to a classroom experience at some time in your life. When the teacher asked a question, it seemed as if half of the students raised their hands before she even finished the question. How could this be? Having spent significant time in classrooms over the course of my life, this behavior mystified me for years. How could they know what they were going to say so quickly? Much later, I finally discovered that the people whose hands instantly shot up were the extraverts. They didn't always know what they were going to say the moment they raised their hands. However, they trusted that the thoughts would form if they were just given the opportunity to speak them. They wanted to be selected so that they could speak—and therefore think—through the answer. That is, an extravert will speak it to think it.

Introverted Thinking

Introverts, on the other hand, prefer that their thoughts be more fully formed *before* they speak. An introvert will sit quietly, listening, pondering, and mulling ideas over in her head, looking for the right word and the best description of the ideas that are taking shape. When I realized that teachers and bosses were judging my participation by the amount that I talked, I wanted to scream, "I am participating! I'm listening."

Introverts form their thoughts internally, and most of the time they are happy to leave them there. They have no compelling need to verbalize their thoughts. Anne Frank captured this preference well when she said, "I've been doing a great deal of thinking, but not saying much."[20]

Unfortunately, this can put introverts at a disadvantage in many classrooms and work situations. In class, as well as in meetings and most social situations, the introverts are the ones who are usually sitting quietly, listening, and thinking. If they raise their hand or speak at all, they will rarely be the first ones to do so. Teachers often misjudge "class participation" based on who raises their hand and speaks in class. Rest assured, the introverts are participating; they're listening and they're thinking. An introvert may look like they are not involved—or worse, look as if they are not interested—when, in fact, the mental wheels are actively spinning.

Leveraging Introverted Thinking

I once had a job in the public sector working for the Pensions Department of the British Government. My boss was one of the most brilliant people for whom I have ever worked. Kenny had come from a top-tier consulting firm. The task before us was a significant transformation project of our large, public-sector IT organization. We faced an endless stream of complex problems to be solved and decisions to be made. These challenges made for frequent, robust conversations.

Kenny was also one of the most extraverted people I have ever met. Ideas would come pouring out of his mouth, emergent and partially formed, at an incredible pace. We would engage in the most intense and stimulating conversations until, inevitably, I would reach a point where I needed more time to process and form my thoughts. While Kenny was talking, I wasn't thinking. I needed to "have a think" as the British like to say. I would bookmark my place in the conversation by saying, "Kenny, I have a brilliant answer for you… and I'll be back in two hours to tell you what it is."

I strongly encourage introverts to put this notion in the top drawer of their communications toolbox. As introverts, it falls on us to teach people how to bring out our best by assuring them that we have more to add to the conversation but that we need more time to process our thoughts. It's important that you deliberately circle back to continue the conversation once you have more to say. When they see that you will return with much more to add, they will begin to encourage you to take the time you need to deepen and formalize your thoughts.

Kenny was an experienced manager and savvy on the differences between introverts and extraverts. He knew that if he let me go away and process my ideas in my optimal way, I would come back and add even more to the conversation. And if, for some reason, I didn't make it back in the promised time, he knew to come looking for me. Savvy extraverts know that there is gold buried in the minds of quiet introverts. Sometimes you must go digging for it.

This lack of understanding between how and where introverts and extraverts think creates one of the greatest underutilized resources in our teams and organizations. Introverts have a tremendous ability to think, process, come up with ideas, and solve problems. Unfortunately, when we assume that everyone thinks in the same fundamental way, many of these ideas remain in the minds of introverts, undeveloped and/or unspoken. The best thinking of introverts and extraverts happens in diametrically opposed environments. Extraverts process deeply in the *presence* of external stimulation, where they can think and verbalize their ideas with other people. Introverts process deeply in the *absence* of external stimulation, especially in the absence of other people talking. Can you see the conflict? When one group is thinking, the other group must essentially shut down their thought processes. Only one of the two ends of the spectrum can function optimally in any one environment.

Not only do introverts need time to incubate their ideas, they generally feel no compulsion to speak them. They are quite happy to leave the thoughts fully formed — but not verbalized — in their minds, available for cross-pollination with new ideas or for connections with dots yet to be discovered. The number of ideas that go unarticulated can be a great loss to teams and relationships.

Socially skilled introverts know how to bridge this gap between introverted and extraverted colleagues. They push themselves to circle back and continue the conversation, adding their thoughts to the group dialogue as they form and mature over time. At the same time, savvy extraverts will know to give introverts the time they need to think and then call on them again (and again) to reveal the ideas that have been forming.

In the workplace these different preferences manifest in myriad ways. An extravert will naturally exhibit a preference for phone calls and face-to-face meetings as their most effective communication format. Their tolerance for long, detailed emails, on the other hand, will be limited. I've seen anecdotes of leaders whose proposed solution to the rising crush of email is to admonish their employees to "just pick up the phone." Some even go as far as declaring email off limits on certain days of the week. Such a company is likely run by a leader with a strong preference for extraversion.

An introvert, on the other hand, will have a stronger preference for email, where they can work out their ideas in advance. Not surprisingly, introverts often have a strong aversion to talking on the phone. Drafting and editing an email allows an introvert to work through his thoughts and more fully organize them before hitting "send." Introverts are famous for composing detailed—and well thought out—emails comprising thousands of words, only to send them to an extravert who sees the density of the text, scans the first paragraph, and picks up the phone to ask for an explanation. If you're an introvert, refrain from email manifestos and white papers when a brief "executive summary" would do. Extraverts, when you receive one of these essays, take the time to read what has been written. You just may be surprised by the brilliance and insight of the email's author.

Compare and Contrast

If an extravert has important work to do, it would not be unusual to hear them say, "Boy, do I ever have a big project to work on. Do you mind if I put some music on?" An introvert in the same situation might say, "Man, I have a big project to work on. Do you mind if I turn the music *off?*" Here are a few more interesting contrasts between introverts and extraverts:

Introverts	Extraverts
Oriented inward	Oriented outward
Reflective, reserved, low-key	Active, congenial
Quiet, calm, enjoy solitude	Enthusiastic, energetic, lively
Thoughts more fully formed before they are spoken	Speak thoughts to form them
Learn by reading, study, reflection, mental practice	Learn from others, by doing
Favor written communications, email	Favor face-to-face communications, telephone
More likely to be introduced than to introduce themselves	Easily connect with other people
Maintain a limited range of relationships	Enjoy associations with a wide variety of people and groups

Caveats and Clarifications

One could spend a lifetime exploring the subtleties and nuances of introversion and extraversion. Because of their relevance to interpersonal relationships, I have focused on just two distinct qualities: how people are energized or stimulated and where people's thought processes take place. Before we delve into how all this applies to networking, a few clarifications are in order.

It's a Spectrum

The differences between the preferences for introversion and extraversion lie along a broad spectrum. In illuminating some of those key differences, I refer to the very ends of the spectrum. Few people fall at these extreme ends. Everyone is, to some degree, an ambivert.

It's a Preference

In Myers-Briggs parlance, introversion and extraversion are preferences, not labels. We do not tag people as introverts or extraverts. Instead, we say that someone has a *preference* for introversion or a *preference* for extraversion. We may even use modifiers, such as, "I have a *strong* preference for introversion," or "He has a *mild* preference for extraversion."

I say this because most people experience a bit of cognitive dissonance when trying to decide where they fall on the introvert-extravert spectrum. We all have moments when we need peace and quiet, and we all have those times when we enjoy being around many people. Everyone can be introverted at some times and extraverted at others. The fact that it's a preference means that we have one underlying default that we tend to rely on more than the other.

It's Contextual

How we present ourselves to the world is highly contextual. Despite our underlying default preference, we learn, over the course of our lives, to adapt to the situations in which we find ourselves. For example, when I moved from the realm of teaching mathematics into the corporate world, I quickly discovered that I had to dial up my extraversion so that I could connect with colleagues more effectively. Similarly, I know introverted parents of extraverted children who have learned to adapt and adjust to the needs of their children. And social situations require all of us to lean into our extraversion at times. It's all contextual.

We Mature Over Time

Everyone has an underlying, default preference point on the introvert-extravert spectrum. When we are young, we operate almost exclusively from that default point. However, as we age—and hopefully mature—we often push ourselves toward the other end of the spectrum. Our natural hunger to grow as human beings leads us to step out of our comfort zones. Introverts become more comfortable with being extraverted, and vice versa.

Network Differently

How do we bring all this background about introverts and extraverts into the realm of networking? Networking is about developing relationships—a deeply personal and human endeavor. Just as there is no predefined way to build a relationship with someone, I offer no predefined ways to network.

The only rule is to be yourself. Be honest and true to where you are along the spectrum of introversion and extraversion.[21] Find ways of socially connecting and relating *that work for you.* Don't try to be what you are not. Don't push yourself to the center of a crowded room if you are more comfortable at the perimeter. Don't feel like you have to pick up the phone if writing an email is how your mind works best. And for goodness' sake, don't try to network the way someone else networks if that approach doesn't feel natural to you. Leverage your preferences. If you are an introvert, network in a way that honors your preferences as an introvert. Ditto for extraverts.

For extraverts, watch out for your propensity to just keep talking. It comes naturally to you, and talking is how you think. But talking too much can take all the oxygen out of the room. In fact, if you find yourself talking too much, the chances are good that you are talking to an introvert. Most introverts are perfectly happy to let you chatter right along. The chance of making any kind of meaningful networking connection when one person does all the talking is nil.

To be a socially skilled extraverted networker, balance your talking with a few good questions and some active listening. Remember that introverts have no inner compulsion to speak their thoughts. It is not natural for them to interrupt. Try to learn about the other person. They may be sitting on a treasure trove of interesting ideas.

For introverts, when you find yourself in networking and social situations, *don't wait to be asked!* Here's an insight gleaned from observing and talking to extraverts over the years: *the extraverts are waiting for you to interrupt.* They're waiting for you to join the conversation. I know you would prefer that your thoughts be more fully formed before speaking them, but conversations don't work that way. Conversations are messy, haphazard, often careening this way and that. Thoughts are only partially formed for everyone. Toss an idea out there and see how it lands. You don't have to move to the center of the room, and you don't have to be the center of attention. But don't just stand there waiting to be asked.

Chapter 4

Why Network?

Having a large fan base is not nearly as important as having a small tribe.

Martin Jones[22]

Before we venture further into our mission to discover a new networking mindset, some may be asking, "Why bother? Do I really need to do this? Is it worth the effort to invest the time and energy it will take to build and maintain a vibrant network?" This is a fair question. Personal and professional networking is over-hyped in our modern media. Everyone and their brother has an idea—and a blog post—about how to network. Most articles offer little more than bromides and misguided advice.

To the networking skeptics, I remind you that humans are social creatures. We have an innate craving to connect with others in meaningful ways. And yet, the more populated our world becomes, the more our traditional sources of social connections are weakening. We barely know our neighbors anymore. Our relationships with our coworkers have not fared much better. It is no coincidence that the very concept of networking has emerged as our lives are becoming more mobile and we increasingly focus our attention online. My hope is that, by the end of this book—if not the end of this chapter—you will see that deliberately building and nurturing a web of personal and professional relationships is a natural extension of who you are and who you aspire to become. Your network becomes part of your identity. I believe that in our modern world, networking is essential. Not networking is not an option.

Don't Grovel

If you are currently employed, you may also be asking yourself, "I already have a job; why would I want to network?" This is one of the more pernicious myths about networking—that networking is for getting a job.

The worst example I have ever encountered of this misguided mindset came years ago when I was participating in a job-search work team.* There were six to eight of us who had decided to meet weekly to support and coach one another in our job searches. During our inaugural meeting we each shared why we were there and what we were hoping to get out of the group. One member said that, while he currently had a job, he was thinking of looking for something else and wanted to "turn up his network." To this day I still can't get that phrase out of my mind. I imagined that this guy thought of his network as akin to a string of Christmas lights. He believed that he could simply light up his network when he needed it and unplug it when he landed a new job. Alas, relationships don't work that way.

It is true that a healthy network is essential to a vibrant career. It is also true that sometimes we need to tap our network for help in that next career move. However, if all we do is ask our network for things, we run the risk that our networking will descend into groveling—or "net-groveling," as I like to call it. We will cover the role of networking as part of a job-search strategy in detail in Chapter 20. And the entire final section on networking inside of your organization is the playbook to networking as a long-term career strategy. Until then, let's explore some other reasons why you might want to network.

---

* If you find yourself searching for a job, joining (or forming) a job-search work team is highly recommended. There are numerous templates for how these teams run, but the basic idea is that team members agree to hold one another accountable for sticking with the arduous task of job searching; you share insights and tips; and you offer support, encouragement, and camaraderie.

Traditional Reasons to Network

Meet Interesting People

My favorite reason to network — and the only reason I ever need — is simply to meet interesting people. We all have a story to tell. The world is full of fascinating people, each of whom have traveled a unique journey. It is amazing what you can learn — especially about yourself — by listening to someone's story.

Knowledge and Information

My second-favorite reason to network might be to learn stuff. Networking can provide a rich source of information on any imaginable subject. What do you need to know? What would you like to learn? Who knows it?

Find Talent

In today's highly specialized and complex world, finding the right person for the job takes more than posting a job description or searching for résumés online. There is a reason that smart companies offer employee referral programs: they work![23] People who network richly can tap into highly qualified talent more easily. As you move through your career, you will find it increasingly valuable to know people who work in your field or industry. Your network becomes a vast pool of potential talent.

A Word About Sales and Business Development

If you have something to sell, ancient wisdom prescribes that you must have a network. Every salesperson knows this. From real-estate agents to global account executives, the oldest reason in the book for active networking is to find new customers, clients, partners, and otherwise mutually beneficial professional relationships. This is classic sales and business development.

However, sales and business development are not networking. Sales-oriented people run the risk of descending into net-groveling if they are not careful. If your only goal is to meet people so that you can sell them something, then you are not exactly embracing the world with a spirit of helpfulness. If you prioritize finding new connections over strengthening existing ones, you may not be networking at all.

That is not to say that sales-oriented people can't also be networking-oriented people. I have met plenty of fantastic salespeople who were also master networkers. The key is to see each connection as a mutually beneficial relationship (not just a potential sale) and to always be looking to offer something of value in exchange for help with whatever you are working on.

Deeper Reasons to Network

Beyond the reasons mentioned above, there are much deeper—and less obvious—reasons to build and nurture a rich web of personal and professional connections.

Your Network Is an Asset

Your network is not just a vast talent pool but also a key asset that belongs uniquely to you. As you mature as a professional and as a leader, it will be increasingly critical to your success that you have a broad network of talent and relationships that you bring with you to each position. Over time your network becomes richer and more valuable. You build it, you maintain it, you leverage it—and no one can take it away from you.

Right Place, Right Time

Successful careers involve a tremendous amount of serendipity. It's not enough to be good at what you do; that's just table stakes. You must also be in the right place at the right time to connect with someone who is willing to pay for the value that you are ready to provide.

Careers do not come with any kind of guarantee of success. However, you can increase your odds substantially by being well networked.

The more active connections in your network, the more likely that you will be in the right place at the right time when opportunities come along.

Karma

Networking with a spirit of helpfulness brings good karma. Traditional networking is self-serving—what's in it for me? The best networkers have always known that there is a "pay-it-forward" aspect to networking. Good things come to those who seek to be helpful and assume other people are doing the same.

Visibility Into the Right Stuff

Networking helps shape your career by offering two-way visibility into what people are working on, and vice-versa. To be successful, you must get four things right:

1. Do good work—this goes without saying, doesn't it?
2. Provide value—in addition to doing good work, you must be doing work that people need. It doesn't matter if you are the best cowpoke in all the land if no one is hiring cowboys anymore.
3. Be visible to others—people must know you and know of you.
4. Have good visibility of others—you must know what other people are working on; what brings value to them, the company, and the marketplace; and what might lie around the next corner.

As we'll see in *Part IV—Networking at Work*, the relationships you build and maintain inside of your organization play an important role in all four of the above steps. It's no longer enough to do good work—if it ever was. To be successful, you must be known. You need a good reputation, a good brand. People need to know what you do, what you aspire to do, what you're working on, and what you're capable of doing. Networking plays a key role in all these things.

Further, modern organizations are complex, multidimensional, and cross-functional. To do your best work, you will need relationships and connections that reach across the organization. Sometimes you will need to draw on your connections to gather or provide information. Other times you will leverage those good relationships to exchange favors or to drive a change through the organization. Networking helps you maintain crucial visibility across the organization over time. This visibility helps you to be recognized as a contributor and may even tip you off about important projects elsewhere in the company.

When you pay attention to what other people are working on, you not only find ways to help them be successful, but you begin to see patterns, which turn into future trends, services, and businesses. You almost automatically adjust and adapt your career trajectory based on what you learn and what provides the most value to the organization (or the market). Networking helps you figure out what this, or any, company will pay you to do. Networking helps you work on the right things and adapt what you do to maximize the value that you can provide.

It Takes a (Global) Village

Perhaps the most important reason of all to network is that success has always required us to be part of a community, a tribe. Your network is your tribe. It is the people to whom you are loyal and who, you trust, will be loyal to you. How you find or build that tribe has evolved considerably over the last few centuries through three distinct identities.

Centuries ago, our tribes were geographic. As we migrated from nomadic lives on the plains and the prairies, we settled in or around small towns. The people of these towns became our tribe. We bought our kitchenware from the local five-and-dime and our shoes from the community cobbler. And, God forbid, if our barn burned down, the entire community came out to help us build a new one. Your tribe, or your "team," was the people in your geographic vicinity. Mutual survival led to mutual success.

In the twentieth century, especially post World War II through the 1990s, more and more people earned their livelihood in ever-larger organizations. We migrated from rural and small-town communities to urban and suburban settings, and we saw the rise of the modern corporation as the place where we earned our livelihoods. It was not uncommon for people to work for one company for a long time — often their entire careers — becoming deeply identified with their coworkers as their "community" or their tribe.

Now, in the twenty-first century, the world has changed again. Geography and physical proximity are no longer the primary factors in determining the organizations we work *for* and, especially, the colleagues we work *with*. Companies are multinational and teams are global. Further, the bond of loyalty between employer and employee has been precipitously weakened. The nature of the employer-employee relationship has evolved beyond the company tribe into a patchwork of contractors, consultants, freelancers, and full-time employees.

The bad news is that your tribe doesn't just come to you with your job or your neighborhood, as it did in the past. The good news is that the rise of communication technology, along with the concomitant emergence of social media, means that we can build our own tribes. Geography be damned! Our networks are no longer constrained by whom we happen to work with and whom we happen to meet in our day-to-day activities. We are free to seek out and build our own personal tribes with whomever and however we choose.

If you want a rich network of mutually beneficial professional relationships, then you must build your own tribe now. The good news is that you get to build the tribe you want. Company and geography no longer bind you. With tools like LinkedIn and Twitter, and a broad array of other social media platforms, technology is minimizing the limitations of geographic separation. We can now create and maintain relationships with people from around the globe who share our interests and passions.

And build them we must. In the modern career, not networking is not an option. Most important, your tribe needs you, the world needs you, and you need your tribe.

Up Next

Let's recap what we've done so far:

- I've made the case for you to have an open mind and an honest assessment of your networking skills.

- I've argued that networking skills are merely a subset of social skills, and both must be learned.

- I've illuminated significant differences between introverts and extraverts and urged you to develop an approach to networking that is true to your personal style and preferences.

- I've argued that there's no one way to network; there are as many approaches to networking as there are people.

- I've made several different cases for why you might want to build a network.

What I haven't done yet is talk about what networking actually is. Let's do that next.

Part II
The Networking Mindset

Chapter 5

Why Mindsets Matter

The great obstacle to discovering the shape of the earth, the continents, and the ocean was not ignorance but the illusion of knowledge.

Daniel Boorstin[24]

Our mindset determines our behavior. How we act is driven by how we think and how we see the world. When it comes to networking mindsets, I have met very few people who have consciously given much thought to their philosophy of networking. Most people just dive right in, assuming that they already know what they are doing or that they will figure it out as they go along. They have a mindset formed by default, gleaned from those around them and based on what seems obvious.

Alas, what seems obvious isn't always so. Behaviors and beliefs that we take for granted often turn out to be ill-founded. Consider one of my favorite examples from history: the heliocentric model of our solar system. For thousands of years up until the late sixteenth century, everyone believed that Earth was the center of the universe. It seemed obvious to them. And they didn't just believe it; they *knew* it to be true. After all, if Earth were moving through space, as Galileo and others eventually started to proclaim, wouldn't we feel it moving? This illusion of knowledge kept scientists and sailors in the dark for countless generations. Except for a few flat-Earth fanatics, we have let go of the mindset that Earth is the center of the universe. And yet, within the entire arc of human history, this is a relatively recent understanding of how our world works.

I believe that many people suffer a similar illusion of knowledge when it comes to networking and professional relationships. We think we know what's true without ever having given it much thought. Networking has become quite popular in the last few decades. Search Meetup.com for any city, and I guarantee that you will find a rich list of groups and events aimed specifically at networking. There is clearly an emerging awareness that networking is important. What we lack, however, is a shared understanding of what it means to network. While there is no shortage of people organizing networking events and talking *about* networking, there are very few people talking about how to *think* about networking.

Our goal here is to remedy that shortfall. In this section we will explore a way of understanding and thinking about networking that will equip us with a robust philosophy and mindset for networking—a mindset that works for all personality types, honors our personal preferences, adapts to our personal styles, and deeply leverages our intrinsic interconnectedness as a society.

Along the way we'll turn a couple of fundamental beliefs about networking upside down. Just as our forefathers were stuck in a geocentric theory of the universe, many modern networkers embrace ideas about networking that just aren't helpful. Most of these networking concepts are not wrong per se; they're just not useful in their current formulation. We'll "flip the bit," as my engineering friends like to say, on a couple of these ideas. The results will provide an approach to networking that makes it natural, comfortable, and powerful.

I invite you to open your mind to the possibility of seeing things differently. Even if you think that you are a good networker, consider that what you think is true just might not be so. Put on your thinking caps and fasten your seatbelts. Here we go.

Chapter 6

What Is a Network?

Ye live not for yourselves; ye cannot live for yourselves; a thousand fibres connect you with your fellow-men, and along those fibres, as along sympathetic threads, run your actions as causes, and return to you as effects.

Henry Melvill[25]

Now that we have cleared away some of the myths about networking, we can answer a deceptively simple question: what is networking?

Have you ever thought about that question? What exactly is networking anyway? Is it going to meetups and networking events? Is it meeting people over coffee or drinks? Is it something you do when you are looking for a job?

I explored this question for a long time. I had a very clear sense of what networking was not: standing in a crowded bar and yelling at someone in a futile attempt to be heard. Nor was it awkwardly engaging in idle small talk that never goes anywhere. The worst non-networking activities are the notorious "speed networking" events. In these well-meaning but eminently ineffective events, people line up on both sides of a long table. At the sound of a bell half of the people start talking — and then shouting — as the decibels quickly escalate to rock-concert levels. You each have sixty seconds to introduce yourself, and this exchange is somehow supposed to lead to life- and career-enriching experiences. Are you kidding me? Is that networking? It never worked for me.

With a growing sense of clarity about what was not networking, I pressed on. What the heck, then, *is* networking? I suppose my background in mathematics feeds my inclination to deconstruct things to their simplest elements, but whenever I find myself stuck on a question for very long, it usually means that I am asking the wrong question. As I stared at the words, "What is networking?" I finally realized that a more fundamental question was staring back at me: what is a *network?*

Now I was getting somewhere. But what, exactly, *IS* a network? Is it people? Is my network the list of contacts in my address book? Is it my connections on LinkedIn or my friends on Facebook? I asked this question to a group of students in Berkeley once, and someone answered, "My network is everyone I have ever met and everyone I ever will."

"Really?" I replied. "You mean my network is everyone I've ever met all the way back to high school? Does it include my childhood friends? As well as everyone I have yet to meet?" While this is a beautiful—and deeply human—sentiment that truly honors our interconnectedness, it's not a very useful definition when it comes to thinking about building a network.

All these notions of a network—a list of contacts, connections on LinkedIn, friends on Facebook—are reasonable and valid. But it turns out that they aren't very helpful. How do I nurture my network if it includes everyone I have ever met? We need a definition of a network that we can put to work, something we can wrap our minds around and use to build a model and philosophy of networking that draws us forward and pulls us together. Thankfully, a more powerful way to define and frame our network has been right in front of us all along.

Active Links

For a better definition of a network, I turned to my engineering friends and my early days in technology when I helped build computer networks. Instead of thinking of a network as comprising just the people—or the "nodes," as the engineers would call them—think of your network as the *connections between* the people. Your network is really the vast array of all the *connections between* you and everyone you know.

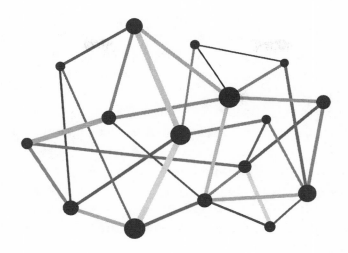

Thinking about your network as the links between you and everyone you know turns out to be a powerful reframing of our human networks. These connections are active, alive with the heartbeat of human relationships. When you take all your connections together, they form a living organism that is imbued with various characteristics, textures, and hues that reflect your personality, while empowering your career and your life.

Key Characteristics of Links

As I delved a little deeper into this concept of active links, I discovered that the individual links between people had two key characteristics that allowed me to visualize my network and unleash the power of networking in my life: freshness and strength.

Freshness

We've all done it: you catch up with an old friend and kick off the conversation by saying, "It's been too long." If you know what I'm talking about, then you already understand that each of the links between you and everyone you know has a degree of freshness. You are meeting and interacting with people all the time—and have been for your entire life. As a result, people ebb and flow in and out of your consciousness. Something may bring them "top of mind" for you, after which time the freshness of that connection immediately begins to fade again. Each time you interact with someone—regardless of whether it's face-to-face, via email or text, by telephone, or through social media—you are freshening the link with that person. For someone you saw this morning or someone you work with every day, the link will be very fresh.

At the other end of the spectrum, you have links that are far from fresh. For someone you haven't seen in years, the link will be quite stale, even dormant. At any given moment, every link between you and everyone you know will have a degree of freshness. Not only is the freshness of a link a natural way to think about relationships, it is also a fundamental component of the way we will think about networking.

Strength

The second useful characteristic that emerges when we think of our network as the *connections between* people, rather than just the people themselves, is that each link also has a certain degree of strength. Relationships are bonds. To be human is to form such bonds with people. Among all the people in your life, you have strong bonds with some people you know, perhaps an old college friend or a similar BFF. It is not unusual for the strength of such links to endure over time, often maintaining much of their strength despite the fact that their freshness fades in the absence of regular attention.

The links are not as strong with other people in your life. Some, like most social media connections, will always have been weak links. Others may have been strong at one time but have atrophied. If you traverse the list of names in your address book, you can quickly see that the strength of the links varies greatly.

Definition of a Network

Now that we have the useful characteristics of freshness and strength to describe the relationship between two people, we can answer the preliminary question on our quest, "What is a network?" A helpful and useful definition turns out to be:

> *Your network is the totality of the connections between you and everyone you know, characterized by the freshness and strength of each of those connections.*

This is the first "bit flip" that I hinted at in the introduction to "Why Mindsets Matter." The emphasis here is on the links between you and the people you know, not just on the people themselves. Your network is a living organism, brought to life by the ebb and flow of the freshness and strength of the connections. It's constantly changing: freshening and fading, strengthening and weakening.

Visualizing Your Network

I am a visual thinker. I believe that it is helpful—and powerful—to think of your network so that you can also picture it in your mind. The concepts of freshness and strength naturally lend themselves to such visualization. Simply imagine the freshness of a link as the physical brightness of the strand. The fresher the link, the brighter the strand. Similarly, visualize the strength of a connection as the thickness of the strand.

Try it! Think of three or four people who you consider to be in your network. Now close your eyes for a moment, and imagine the links between you and these people so that the freshness of the connection is reflected by how *bright* the link is. Can you see it? Can you see the various strands of light between you and these people, each with varying degrees of brightness? Now add the image of the thickness of those strands as well. Extend this visualization to the hundreds of people you know. Can you see it? Can you see the living, evolving, morphing, interconnected web of relationships that is your network?

So far so good. We now have a useful definition of a network: the collection of links between you and everyone you know, characterized by the freshness and strength of each link. It's a good definition because it's a helpful definition. It points the way forward for how we might want to act. For example, the fact that the freshness of a link fades over time invites us to action. Onward on our quest to understand networking.

Exercise: Network Analysis

Strategically reviewing your professional relationships on a regular basis is a critical part of building and maintaining a powerful network, and an integral component of your overall networking activity. It's as much a part of networking as meeting face-to-face or corresponding with people. I strive go through my entire list of LinkedIn connections at least twice a year in this manner, reviewing what people are currently up to, looking for links that I wish were fresher or stronger, and planning activities that will help me realize those wishes.

Step 1

Thinking of your network as a collection of links and connections is a novel way to think about the web of relationships you have built over your career. I recommend taking a moment to practice this new way of thinking.

Take out a piece of paper and divide it into four sections:*

- Fresh Links
- Not-So-Fresh Links
- Strong Connections
- Not-So-Strong Connections

Think of at least three people you know for each section. The names of people with fresh links and strong connections should come easily. For example, under "Fresh Links," list the names of three people

---

* All of the exercises in this book are included in *The Workbook of Helpful Exercises*, which can be downloaded at **heatherhollick.com/helpful**.

with whom you have met recently—perhaps someone you met with today or in the last few days. Under "Strong Connections" think of three people with whom the connections are particularly strong for you—perhaps a partner, an old boss, a childhood friend.

The names for "Not-So-Fresh" and "Not-So-Strong" will take a little bit more work—if they were top of mind, they probably wouldn't be in this category to begin with. Pull up your address book and peruse the names until you come up with three names for each section.

Step 2

Go through your entire list of LinkedIn connections and assess each link's degree of freshness and strength. Rate both the freshness and strength of each connection on a scale of 1 to 5, where 1 is not fresh or not strong and 5 is super fresh or super strong. Note those links that you would like to see fresher or stronger.

Now look through your ratings and decide if anything needs to change. Are there some low numbers that you wish were higher? Are there faded links that you wish were fresher? Are there weak links that you wish were stronger?

Chapter 7

What Is Networking?

Real power comes from being indispensable.
Indispensability comes from being a switchboard, parceling
out as much information, contacts, and goodwill to as many
people — in as many different worlds — as possible.

Keith Ferrazzi[26]

At last we are ready to answer the question that started us on this quest in the first place: what is networking?

If you follow the logic that we have been building up to this point, then you already have a good sense of what networking must be. With our definition of a network based on the freshness and strength of the links between you and everyone you know, the act of networking practically defines itself. Networking must be *anything* that *freshens* or *strengthens* a *link* with someone.

For the sake of a complete networking definition, we must allow for the reality of meeting new people and adding them to our network as well. Hence, in addition to freshening and strengthening links, our definition of networking must include the act of *creating* links as well. This leads us to a powerful definition of networking:

> Networking is any activity that creates,
> freshens, or strengthens a relationship
> between you and another person.

That's it! After all those ineffective networking events and countless occasions of standing almost catatonic in a noisy bar trying to hear someone speak, I finally found an answer to the question, "What is networking?" Networking is simply the act of creating, freshening, or strengthening a relationship with someone.

More Than Just Meeting New People

Some will be surprised by this definition of networking. Many people think of networking as the act of meeting *new* people. While creating new connections is certainly a part of networking, it is a very small part of the overall effort you must exert over the course of your life to build and maintain a vibrant web of professional relationships. The bulk of your time and energy should be directed to the care and feeding of your *existing* network—it is, after all, a living organism. Most of your networking efforts should be invested in freshening and strengthening the links with the people who you already consider to be in your network.

Make It Personal

The beauty of defining networking as the act of creating, freshening, and strengthening links is that it customizes networking to your personality, style, and preferences. Networking is about building relationships, and building relationships is a deeply personal and human endeavor. As you think about networking activities—and especially as you consider networking events—it is critically important that you expand your concept of networking according to our new definition and then choose networking activities that work *for you*.

When I think about engaging in networking, I strive to put myself in situations where I can present my best self. For me, these are usually one-on-one or small-group situations. For others, it may be organized network events. The point is that networking is about building and maintaining a web of relationships. To do that, you need to be genuine, authentic, and engaged. I can't do that if I am trying to network the way someone else networks. I am at my best when I honor my preferences and my personal style.

The importance of adapting your networking activities to your personality cannot be overstated. Any activity that creates, freshens, or strengthens relationships *for you* is networking *for you*. On the other hand, anything that does not create, freshen, or strengthen relationships *for you* is not networking *for you!*

Let me repeat that. *Anything* that creates, freshens, or strengthens relationships *for you* is networking *for you*. And, conversely, any activity that does not create, freshen, or strengthen relationships *for you* is not networking *for you!*

I once received an invitation for an event held at a baseball stadium that was billed as "The World's Largest Networking Event." As a person with a strong preference for introversion and a hypersensitivity to the din of large crowds, I cannot imagine an atmosphere where I would be less likely to create, freshen, or strengthen a link with anyone. I did not attend, knowing that no networking would have taken place that evening *for me!*

Similarly, you have permission to never stand in a noisy bar or overcrowded hall again in the name of networking if that doesn't work for you. You know the environments I am talking about — the ones where the cacophony of voices shouting to make themselves heard reaches decibel levels akin to standing twenty feet away from a roaring jet engine.

Never mind the utter futility of trying to build or nurture a relationship in such an environment, the overstimulation in these settings drives the cortisone levels of most introverts off the charts. I am not presenting my best self when my anxiety levels are so high. Even though such gatherings are often billed as networking events, I usually avoid them, safe in the knowledge that my preferences and networking style preclude creating, freshening, or strengthening any links *for me* in these environments.

I'm not saying that it is impossible to network at such events. I know plenty of people who find such environments highly stimulating and do well in creating, freshening, and strengthening relationships at them. Nor can I say that I never attend such events. Sometimes social obligations — or the prospect of a good beverage — sway me into attending. But I don't kid myself into believing that *I* am doing any networking there. For me, if I can't hear myself think, I can't build relationships with people. And if I can't build or nurture relationships, then I am not networking. It's as simple as that.

Chapter 8

Creating Links

There are no strangers here; only friends you haven't yet met.

Edgar A. Guest[27]

Let's delve a little deeper into the aspects of creating, freshening, and strengthening links. How does one go about adding new links and new relationships to your network? The short answer is that we expand our networks both passively and actively. Or, stated another way, we create new links through luck and through intention.

Creating Links Through Serendipity

For most of us, the default—and often only—way that we add new relationships to our network is through chance, good fortune, and happy accidents. We encounter new people every day, at work, at play, at the supermarket, at networking events. Some of these people make it into our network; some don't. Not everyone we meet is a candidate for our tribe. Far from it. Only a small portion of these chance encounters intrigues us enough to invest the effort to incorporate the person into our network.

Sometimes people are sent our way. On a good day, other people in our network will send us new potential connections by way of an introduction. It's always a pleasant surprise when an email pops into my inbox from one of my network connections saying, "I really think you two should connect." Whether I find them or they find me, I would guess that about half of the people in my network got there through chance encounters and serendipity.

Creating Links With Intention

For the most successful professionals, networking is primarily an intentional, deliberate activity. While it is always a treat to meet someone unexpectedly and realize that they would be a valuable addition to your network, you can't build a network — and a career — based solely on people who passively come your way. Further, once you identify someone as a good candidate for your network, it requires deliberate effort to build and nurture a relationship with them. Smart networkers understand that their network is too important to leave solely to chance.

To build your network with intention, take an active stance by seeking out people who will complement and augment what you have to offer and who you aspire to be. Look for people who can help you achieve your work, life, and career goals. Which personality types are a good fit for you? Which industries and professions align with your aspirations as well as your career? What are some of your core values? Which kinds of people reflect these core values?

With a clear sense of the *kinds* of people that you want in your network, start exploring where you might connect with some of these people. Which activities can you participate in that would increase the likelihood that you will meet one (or more) of these people?

For example, I love people who march to their own drum and may be a bit rough around the edges when it comes to commonly accepted social skills. And I have always been drawn to creatives — artists, designers, musicians, photographers, and so forth. As a result, I often make a deliberate effort to add such people to my network.

Similarly, I place high value on people who have lived and traveled to other places. And I have deep admiration for people who have earned advanced degrees, whatever their field of study. Most of all, I value diversity of thought. I look for people who think differently than I do — people with different perspectives and frames of reference. The broader and more diverse your network becomes, the more valuable it is to you and the people in it. When I meet people who resonate with these values and interests, I make an effort to create a network connection with them.

Creating Links by Scanning Your Field of View

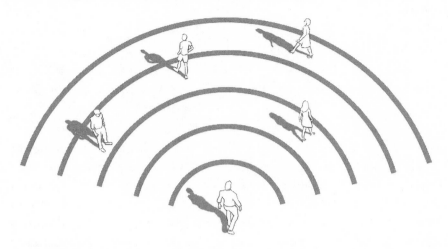

Successful networking involves forward motion. Imagine your career as if you were driving a car. Looking out the windshield, you can see the road ahead as it races toward you. But with very little effort you can also look to the left and to the right to take in a broad field of view. An important aspect of deliberately seeking out people that you want in your network is to look in the direction you are headed with your career and see who lies in your field of view.

Ask yourself, "What kind of people do I need in my network to enhance my opportunities and my experience as I travel on this path?" If you look ahead to where you want to be in one year, three years, five years from now, what kind of people do you need in your life to help make that happen? Seek out those people.

Be Aspirational

In addition to adding people to your tribe through serendipity, intention, and looking along your career trajectory, the final way to add people to your network is to think big. I follow the lead of Keith Ferrazzi on maintaining an aspirational contact list. In his highly recommended book *Never Eat Alone,* he explains,

There's another category you might want to add, something I call my "aspirational contacts." There are those extremely high-level people who have nothing to do with my business at hand but are just, well, interesting or successful or both. The people on that list may be anyone from heads of state and media moguls, to artists and actors, to people others speak highly of. I list these people, too.[28]

Your aspirational contact list is not about celebrities you admire or heroes you worship. It's aspirational in the sense that it fuels *your* aspirations as well. It's a list of people you want to be part of your network, not just a roster of people you want to meet. You aspire not only to meet them but to also *grow yourself and build your network* so that they will be glad to have you in *their* network if you ever get the opportunity to connect with them.

For each person on your aspirational contact list, ask yourself, "What do I need to know or do to be ready to meet this person?" If the answer is "nothing," then this is not an aspirational contact. Work your network now and figure out a way to get an introduction.

If, however, you feel like you are not quite ready to meet this person, let the gap be aspirational. What do you need to do to be ready?

- Perhaps you need to bolster your reputation in your field, publish an article or two, or speak at a conference.
- Is there something you need to learn? A new skill? Perhaps a new certification?
- Are you running with the right crowd? Who else should be in your network before you reach out to meet this person?

Aspirational contacts can be great role models, inspirations, and motivations to move our lives and careers forward. They can also be great network connections once you get there.

Chapter 9

Freshening Links

Hello old friend
It's really good to see you once again.

Eric Clapton

Before we delve into techniques for freshening our network links, let's unpack the fact that links need to be freshened at all. Once again, I'll borrow from the world of technology. In computer networks, while you are interacting with your computer in the foreground—surfing the web, watching videos, reading emails, or posting on Facebook—packets of data are constantly being exchanged between the computers in the background. One such background packet is the keepalive. Wikipedia explains it well:

> A keepalive (KA) is a message sent by one device
> to another to check that the link between the two is
> operating, or to prevent the link from being broken... A
> keepalive signal is often sent at predefined intervals,
> and plays an important role on the Internet. After a
> signal is sent, if no reply is received the link is assumed
> to be down and future data will be routed via another
> path until the link is up again. A keepalive signal
> can also be used to indicate to Internet infrastructure
> that the connection should be preserved.[29]

Well said. To keep our human networks vibrant, we need the interpersonal equivalent of a keepalive.

Links Fade

I think of the freshness of a link in my network as having a half-life, in much the same way that radioactive elements decay. For me and my network, the half-life of a connection's freshness is about three months. Suppose I meet with someone for a cup of coffee this morning.

- In three months' time the freshness of that link will be about one-half as fresh as it was the moment that we bid adieu.
- In three more months, the freshness will be one-fourth (½ x ½).
- After nine months it will be one-eighth (½ x ½ x ½).
- And a year after the time we had our last cup of coffee together, the freshness of that connection will have decayed four half-lives. That is, the freshness of the connection will be down to one-sixteenth of its original freshness (½ x ½ x ½ x ½).

On the human scale that seems about right. One-sixteenth is a small number. If you think about a light that has faded to one-sixteenth of its original brightness, that's pretty dim. And so it is with the freshness of links between two people who are separated by time.

Relationship Management

At this point you should be pushing back at me. You should be protesting, "Look, I understand that the freshness of each link fades over time, but you can't possibly expect me to keep all of the connections in my network fresh?" You are right. You can't.

Once again, I will tap into the wisdom of Keith Ferrazzi and his insights in *Never Eat Alone*.[30] According to Ferrazzi's system of level 1, 2, or 3 contacts, the trick is to think of your network as a set of concentric circles of people with whom you are maintaining a mutually beneficial relationship.

Monthly

The innermost circle contains the people with whom you would like to stay in touch on a monthly basis. It's not necessary to email or call *every single person* in the inner circle *every single month,* although I tried that for a while. It's more a way of qualifying the value you currently place on the relationship.

The way that I think of it now is this: if more than a month goes by without contact or communication, I should reach out. These people are in my current inner circle. I don't need to make an excuse to freshen the connection. My inner circle often includes people I've just met and want to follow up with to ground the relationship at the beginning. It may also include people with whom I am currently doing busi-

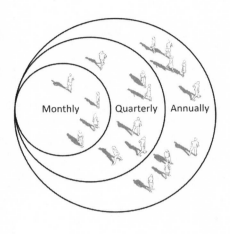

ness. Mostly, my inner networking circle includes the people I value dearly. Either of us may take the initiative to connect as we are mutually committed to keeping the connection fresh.

The size of the inner circle varies widely over time and from person to person. It depends on what you are currently doing, where you are on the spectrum of introversion and extraversion, and where you are in your life.

Quarterly

The next concentric circle in our network contains the people to whom, if more than a quarter of a year has gone by, you will not hesitate to reach out. This may be people you know well, and a quarterly "keep-alive" is sufficient for each of you to keep the other person top of mind.

Annually

The list of annual contacts forms the largest networking circle for most people. These may be your casual acquaintances or the people for whom time and circumstances limit both parties from more frequent communications.

Birthdays are a great time to freshen links with people in your network. I make every effort to record the dates of people's birthdays in my personal address book and on my calendar so that I can see their birthday coming *before* their special day arrives. I send handwritten birthday cards if I have their mailing address and a heartfelt email on the morning of their birthday if I do not. The one thing that I do not do on someone's birthday is chime in with the chorus of birthday greetings on LinkedIn or Facebook. My interest is in freshening a relationship with someone in my network. Getting lost in the streaming barrage of well-wishers sending birthday emojis on social media will do little to accomplish that.

Like birthdays, holiday seasons are a wonderful time to refresh connections with people in the annual circle of your network. I still enjoy sending (and receiving) handwritten Christmas cards through the mail. Some years I send a heartfelt email on New Year's Day. Whether you send an annual holiday newsletter or go so far as to send gifts, the holiday season can be the perfect time to refresh connections with those in your annual networking circle.

Archives and Everyone Else

As you regularly scrub through your contact list, you will find that some people don't fit in any of your current networking circles. Their lives may have moved in a direction different from yours, and there is no longer a mutually beneficial reason to stay in touch. That's okay. In fact, it's very important to review and trim your network on a regular basis. Not every name that has found its way into your address book will be in one of your network circles. It's hard to imagine that a network that includes everyone you've ever met is really a network at all. People move on. So should you.

No Statute of Limitations

People often wonder if there is a protocol for freshening links that have long faded. Thankfully, there is no statute of limitations on reviving mutually beneficial relationships. I have received the most heartwarming "getting back in touch" emails, and I have sent more than a few myself.

If there is a networking connection that you would like to bring back to life, reach out to them. I recommend sending an email — or better yet, a card* — that begins by expressing how important they are to you and that you have been remiss in letting so much time go by without telling them so. Proceed to bring them up to speed on where you are in your life and what you're working on now. Inquire the same about them. And then, for goodness' sake, don't let so much time go by again without doing something to freshen or strengthen the link.

Techniques for Freshening Links

Again, networking is a deeply personal endeavor. How *you* freshen *your* network connections will be unique to you, your preferences, your style, your circumstances, and the people in your network. Here, however, are a few suggestions.

Face-to-Face

The most powerful and effective way to freshen a connection with someone is to meet them face-to-face. Face-to-face connections can be over lunch, coffee, dinner, or drinks. They can be an intimate one-on-one conversation over a meal or a brief chat in the halls of a conference center.

While human relationships flourish in the rich environment of in-person connections, it is important to acknowledge that such encounters are expensive when it comes to our time. There are only so

---

* I realize that sending a written communication is the first impulse of an introvert. However, to revive a faded relationship, I recommend it for the extraverts as well. The key is to express in the opening paragraph why you are reconnecting. Those kinds of things are hard to say right out of the gate in a verbal conversation.

many hours in a week, and in our crazy, busy, over-scheduled worlds, many of those hours are already spoken for. It is often difficult to prioritize the time for such meetings. I recommend being realistic. Building and nurturing my network is important, but I usually reserve face-to-face meetings for people in my inner circle and for new contacts I am just getting to know. Similarly, I am respectful of other people's time when I suggest opportunities to meet with them.

Electronic Communications

Modern technology makes the modern network possible. Emails, phone calls, voice mail, and instant messages are the sweet spot of keeping network connections fresh. Extraverts often prefer phone calls or voice mail. As an introvert, my first inclination is usually to send an email. I find that a monthly or quarterly email is always warmly received and not difficult to create. The format is almost down to a template for me:

- The subject line will usually say "Checking in"
- The opening line will say something about how long it has been since we connected and how I value keeping the connection alive.
- The second paragraph will recap what we talked about the last time we connected. "The last time we talked you were… How is that going?" If it has been too long, I may refer to their LinkedIn profile and ask them how things are going based on the information they have posted there.
- The third paragraph will offer an update of where I am and what I'm working on.
- Finally, I will close with a request for them to update me on what they're working on.

Almost invariably I get a response within a few hours acknowledging the connection and updating me on what they are working on. If I can think of some way to be helpful, I act on it. In any case, this is networking at its finest: two interconnected souls, separated by geography, refreshing their human connection through the miracle of (relatively) modern technology.

Finally, in the realm of electronic communications, text and messaging apps are perfect for spur-of-the-moment exchanges and pings,* especially for people in your inner circle.

Social Media

Social media can play both an active and a passive role in our networking lives. In an active role, social media is a fast and easy way to communicate short snippets with a broad pool of people. Updating your timeline on Facebook, sending a tweet, or publishing a status update on LinkedIn is a quick way to inform your network of what you're thinking about or what you're working on.

Social media can also play a valuable passive role in your networking strategy. Social media is a great way to "listen to your network." As we'll see shortly, networking is about understanding what people are working on and finding ways to be helpful. People's profiles, their online presence, and their activity on social media all tell a story. You can learn a lot about who a person is and what they are working on by viewing their LinkedIn profile, reading their tweets, and following their updates.

However, don't fool yourself into thinking that you're getting more networking mileage from your social media activity than you really are. Spending time on social media is no substitute for investing time and energy in building and nurturing mutually beneficial relationships. Sociologists and cultural anthropologists call social media connections "weak links" or "weak ties" — and for good reason. Sending a tweet or making a comment on Facebook registers pretty low on the scale of human interactions; they are a keepalive at best. Furthermore, while everyone is talking on social media, I'm not sure anyone is actually

---

* "Ping" in this sense comes from the world of computer networking, where the term derives from the interaction of a computer user sending a small packet of data to a remote computer to determine whether there is a connection. It is the manual version of the keepalive.

listening. As gratifying—and addicting—as it can be, amassing a following on social media is a far cry from building your tribe.

We'll delve much deeper into leveraging social media as both an active and passive networking tool in *Part III—Networking in Action*.

Friends vs. Network Connections

People often wonder if they should consider their friends as part of their network. After all, isn't your network a professional thing? Should your career network be distinct from your friends?

We've gone to great lengths to define what we mean by a network and by networking. Our framing of a network is built upon the idea of a web of mutually beneficial relationships characterized by the freshness and strength of each relationship. As we have said, your network is your tribe, the people to whom you are loyal and who, you trust, are loyal to you. In this definition, your friends are absolutely a part of your network. You should be as invested in leveraging who and what you know to help them be successful as you would for anyone in the professional branches of your network.

The inverse, whether everyone in your network is also your friend, hinges on the definition of a friend, a subject much too deep for this journey.

Chapter 10

Strengthening Links

The bond that links your true family is not one of blood,
but of respect and joy in each other's life.

Richard Bach[31]

A good network has a healthy blend of both strong *and* weak connections. In the age of social media, it's too easy to have a preponderance of *weak* links in your network. In fact, left undeveloped, most network connections never move beyond a weak link. The challenge—and the art—of building a powerful network is to know how and when to invest in a relationship to forge it into a *strong* connection.

Strong links between people develop in the context of a broad range of factors, spanning everything from shared interests to networking savvy to geographic proximity. You never know in advance which connections can—or should—become strong connections for you. The key is to be alert. Always be on the lookout for people who are looking for you. While an avid networker will constantly be scanning the horizon for opportunities to *freshen* any connection, weak or strong, the key to becoming a truly skilled networker is also to concurrently look for opportunities to *strengthen* some of them as well. Your network is an asset that takes on real power when you deliberately and selectively invest to strengthen some of your connections.

How, exactly, does one set out to strengthen relationships? Don't strong bonds between people just emerge over time? Through shared experience? Yes, they do. But living, working, and pursuing a career *are* shared experiences. Further, you don't need a lot of common ground to share a strong relationship with someone. Some of the most powerful connections occur when people and ideas come together from completely different spheres. If you're listening — and paying attention — to the depth and breadth of your network, your network will offer you countless ways to quickly build trust and strengthen even fledgling relationships.

The essence of building strong relationships is simply to embrace the world with a spirit of helpfulness. Be on the lookout for ways to be helpful. Opportunities abound. When you see an opportunity, offer to do a favor or extend a gesture of goodwill.

You have more to offer than you know. You've been around. You know things — and you know people. If you can find a way to share who and what you know with people, you will be helpful. Get to know the other person and connect some dots. Help them solve a problem they are working on. Find a way to share what you know, or leverage your network to make an introduction.

Keith Ferrazzi, a master networker by any measure, calls it social arbitrage, which he defines as "the constant exchange of favors and information." The word "arbitrage" conveys a sense of ruthlessness to me that doesn't quite fit with the spirit of networking. I prefer to call it social amplification. In any case, Ferrazzi explains it this way:[32]

> *It's a sort of career karma. How much you give to the people you come into contact with determines how much you'll receive in return. In other words, if you want to make friends and get things done, you have to put yourself out to do things for other people — things that require time, energy, and consideration.*
>
> *Successfully connecting with others is never about simply getting what you want. It's about getting what you want and making sure that people who are important to you get what they want first. Often, that means fixing up people who would otherwise never have an opportunity to meet.*

How It Works

Imagine you are meeting someone for the first time, perhaps at some sort of networking event. What is going through your mind during the first few moments of conversation? If you are unskilled at networking, you might be asking yourself, "What can this person do for me?" The problem with this approach is that it is egocentric, and it does nothing to strengthen the relationship.

But if you are a skilled networker, you're not thinking about yourself first. Instead, you're asking yourself, "How can I be helpful to this person? Who do I know and what do I know that could help them be successful?" Whenever you are interacting with someone in a professional capacity, just keep these questions running through your mind on an endless loop:

> *Who do I know...*
> *What do I know...*
> *that could help this person be successful?*
>
> *Who do I know...*
> *What do I know...*
> *that could help this person on their journey*
> *to wherever they are headed?*
>
> *Who do I know...*
> *What do I know...*
> *that would be useful to this person?*

This is the second "bit flip" that I promised above. Most people engage in networking from the perspective of, "What's in it for me?" (WIIFM). Others seem to engage in networking without thinking at all. I urge you to put yourself in the elite category of networkers who understand the interconnectedness of success and seek first to be helpful to others. Do what you can to help people get where they are trying to go—even if the other person isn't exactly clear on where that is. A skilled networker thinks about networking and professional relationships as an opportunity to be helpful. They are constantly thinking of ways to leverage their skills, knowledge, and connections to that end.

And what will be the return on such generous and benevolent investments in your fellow sojourners along your respective career paths? Soon you will begin to surround yourself with like-minded people. The good will that you generate from the constant exchange of favors and information has a way of resonating throughout your network. Further, a spirit of helpfulness has a way of amplifying and making its way full-circle back to you. You will find yourself both the custodian and the beneficiary of a vibrant and powerful network.

Don't Be Afraid to Ask

The guiding principle of this book is to engage the world with a spirit of helpfulness. When you find a way to do a favor for someone, it strengthens the relationship. You feel grateful that you were able to help. You feel a little bit more alive for having made even a small impact on someone else's life. You feel a few of the sinewy strands of the relationship strengthened.

The inverse is also true, sometimes even more so. When you ask a favor of someone else and they oblige, you not only feel more connected to them, but they also feel a stronger bond to you. Both of you are more likely to exchange favors and information in the future.

The power of asking for a favor has become known as the Ben Franklin Effect. Steve Dalton, a senior career consultant at Duke University's Fuqua School of Business and author of *The 2-Hour Job Search*, describes the phenomenon beautifully in an article he wrote for *The Huffington Post*:

> The Ben Franklin Effect is named after an anecdote
> Franklin recounted from his early political days.
> In 1737, while running for reappointment as Clerk
> in Philadelphia's General Assembly, a wealthy
> and influential new member passionately argued
> (unsuccessfully) for a different candidate. Franklin

wanted this new member's advocacy for himself, so, upon learning that the new member possessed a rare book collection, Franklin asked to borrow one of his most valuable books. The new member obliged, and Franklin read and returned the book a week later with a note acknowledging the favor, but nothing else.

Upon seeing each other at the next meeting, the new member initiated a conversation with Franklin for the first time and offered his assistance on any future occasion. He honored this promise until his death, prompting Franklin to acknowledge the truth of an old maxim he had heard: "He that has once done you a kindness will be more ready to do you another, than he whom you yourself have obliged." In social psychology, this concept is now called the Ben Franklin Effect.[33]

Recap

We've come a long way from that initial question, "What is networking?" To recap, networking is a three-pronged activity: creating, freshening, and strengthening links between you and other people. Anything that creates, freshens, or strengthens a link *for you* is networking. And anything that does not create, freshen, or strengthen a link *for you*—regardless of how effectively those things might work for other people—is not networking *for you*.

You create links, i.e., new relationships, with people through both serendipitous encounters and intentional network-building. A network is too important to leave to chance, so you strategically look for people you want in your network and find ways to meet them.

Freshening links is a deliberate act that amounts to the care and feeding of your network. You freshen links through countless ways that fit your personality, your lifestyle, your career ambitions, and your network.

And finally, you strengthen links with a select subset of people in your network through a constant exchange of favors and information. Sometimes you initiate the exchange; other times you ask for a favor. Either way, you make investments in some of your networking relationships in order to strengthen them or keep them strong.

Chapter 11

The Ultimate
Networking Question

*You can have everything in life you want, if you will
just help other people get what they want.*

Zig Ziglar

We now know that networking is about creating, freshening, and strengthening links with people. And we know that strengthening links is accomplished through the constant exchange of favors and information. But what does that really mean? How do we work with that? Beyond the vague notion of embracing the world with a spirit of helpfulness, how do we enact the power of strengthening links? How do you figure out what kind of favor to offer? Or ask for? How do you know what information the other person might find helpful?

Put simply, you ask them. You don't ask them directly, mind you. That rarely nets any kind of useful exchange. A good networker figures out ways to be helpful indirectly and in a way that draws the relationship forward.

Your first inclination might be to pose the straightforward question, "How can I help you?" This might work if the person to whom you are talking has sought you out and knows exactly what they want. In such a case, they may have reached out to you because they are looking for a specific introduction or a particular piece of advice.

But most networking situations are not so well defined, and most networkers are not so well prepared. Often the people you meet will have only the vaguest sense of what they want or need in their lives.

Further—and this is the crux of the challenge—they don't know what or who you know. They have no way of knowing the depths of what you have to offer. As a result, in most cases they have no idea how best to respond to your straightforward inquiry, "How can I help you?"

Besides, the question "How can I help you?" can be a bit off-putting in casual conversations. Expecting people to *ask you* for what they need can come off as a bit haughty.

There's a better way to engage people and find out how you might be helpful. Instead of expecting people to know what to ask us for, we are going to develop a conversational technique that invites the other person to open up about a challenge or a project they are working on. Then we will use our knowledge of our network to look for ways to be helpful.

Before we do that, we need to take a brief jaunt through the world of small talk. It turns out that you can't just jump into a deep conversation with someone and start exploring how to be helpful. Personal boundaries and social customs in most cultures require that we ease our way into deeper, more meaningful conversations, if the conversation ends up going deeper at all.

A Word About Small Talk

I used to hate small talk—most introverts do. I just couldn't understand the point of superficial, inane conversations that never went anywhere on vacuous topics that no one could possibly care about. Sure, I have the usual interest in the weather and a fleeting interest in sports, but do we have to talk about them? For the longest time I couldn't figure out what could be gained by talking about them.

My dislike of small talk was exacerbated by my feeling that I was comically bad at it. Most of my attempts were characterized by awkward phrases and even more awkward pauses. I would stumble and mumble like Lieutenant Columbo trying to strike up a conversation with Adrian Monk.

And then I made two discoveries:

1. I was not alone. Everybody stumbles and bumbles their way through small talk.

2. Small talk plays a vital role in initiating conversations. There was, indeed, a lot that could be gained from small talk.

Weary of my perceived ineptitude at starting conversations, I decided to collect some data. For several months I paid close attention to how other people conducted the opening volley of a conversation. Whenever I was within earshot of two people initiating a conversation, I listened and watched closely, observing both their words and their body language. Here is a composite of a typical exchange between two people:

Person A: "Hey, how you doin'?"

Person B: "Great, how about you?"

Person A: "I'm doing well. 'sup?"

Person B: "Not much, what's up with you?"

And so it would go. Sometimes these frivolous exchanges ended up going somewhere meaningful; other times they fell flat, remaining in the realm of the superficial and mundane.

I was amazed to discover how hit-or-miss most small talk encounters were. Even the ones that worked tended to start out like bumper cars at the kids' carnival. What a relief it was to discover that real life wasn't like an Aaron Sorkin script,[*] where everyone fires witty and sharp retorts in rapid succession.

It wasn't that I was particularly bad at small talk after all. There is no "good" or "bad" when it comes to small talk. Small talk just *is*. And small talk is almost always this strange — sometimes surreal — exchange

---

[*] Aaron Sorkin is an American screenwriter, playwright, director, and producer. While I love everything I have seen by him, his defining works for me are the movie *A Few Good Men* and the television series *The West Wing*. These shows, *The West Wing* in particular, feature scene after scene in which the characters exchange lines of dialogue that are witty, erudite, and dense. While it is a joy to watch consummate actors deliver beautifully written and meticulously rehearsed lines, real-life conversations rarely come close to this.

between two people who are subconsciously negotiating how they will communicate. It may or may not move on to a more substantial conversation.

A Salute to Fax Machines

So, if small talk just *is*, what's the point? To answer this question, I discovered a surprising analogy between small talk and the now-ancient world of fax machines and computer modems. Have you heard the sound that two computer modems or fax machines would make when they were first connecting?* If not, I invite you to follow the link in the footnotes to hear a recording.

After the dial tones of the initiating modem and the screeching "hello" of the remote machine answering, the two devices would squawk and squelch at each other in an ear-melting array of notes and tones for fifteen or twenty seconds. Then both machines would go silent, and the exchange of information would ensue.

Do you know what was going on during those initial moments of cacophony? The telecommunications engineers who made the whole thing possible called it "handshaking." They defined those twenty seconds of what sounds like cacophony to the untrained ear as "an automated process of negotiation that dynamically sets parameters of a communications channel established between two entities before normal communication over the channel begins."[34]

As fax machines and computer modems emerged and evolved, the "language" they spoke, also known as "protocols," evolved as well. Different fax machine and modem manufacturers developed competing protocols, and standards evolved quickly. The first thing the two machines had to do was figure out if they could communicate with each other. They were trying to find a common language.

Further, the quality of the phone lines varied dramatically. This variation in line quality meant that the speed at which data could be transmitted varied significantly as well. Hence, before two machines could

---

* To hear the sounds that modems make while negotiating a connection — or to just take a trip down memory lane — go to bit.ly/helpful_modem and enjoy thirty seconds of retro aural delight.

connect and exchange any kind of meaningful information, they had to settle on two things:

1. What language (if any) can we speak?
2. If we do find a common language, what is the quality of our connection?

This computer handshaking is the perfect analogy for the human interactions we call small talk. Whenever two people first attempt to interact in conversation, there is a short, subtle negotiation around *if* and *how* they might communicate. Just like the computer modems, during the opening volley of seemingly inane conversations people are answering such questions as, "Can we communicate?" "If so, how?" "At what level will we connect?" "What will be the mood and tone of our conversation?" "Will we be serious or jocular?" "Shallow or deep?"

This negotiation all takes place on a subconscious level and within the same fifteen to twenty seconds that computer modems need to establish a connection. If we manage to "get on the same wavelength," a conversation is possible. We negotiate for a few seconds, and then we either dive into the conversation or we move on. Thus, the role of small talk is to ascertain whether we will be able to communicate, and if so, how. It turns out be indispensable and vital to any conversation.

This kind of negotiation at the beginning of a conversation is ubiquitous. It occurs not only with people we have just met but also with people we know well—pretty much every time we see them. The initial volley—for example, "How was your day?"—helps both parties determine the ensuing mood and tone of the conversation. You can't communicate meaningfully without first settling on *how* you will communicate.

Try observing this on your own. First, take the opportunity to eavesdrop on the initial volleys of conversations taking place near you in public. Notice how the two participants subconsciously navigate how and what they are going to talk about.

Next, observe your own instances of small talk, especially with someone close to you. Notice how you tend to automatically match the tone of the other person in mere seconds after the conversation begins. That is the power of small talk.

I no longer hate small talk. Now it just makes me smile. I've learned to see small talk as the opening volley of a potentially meaningful conversation. Small talk allows me to align with another person as we prepare for a possible exchange of favors and information. That is an amazing power. Small talk is now my friend.

Prepare to Be Spontaneous

Preparing to be spontaneous may sound oxymoronic but, I assure you, it is not. Because of the important role of small talk in initiating conversations and because, as an introvert, I prefer that my thoughts be more fully formed before I speak them, I invest time and energy keeping abreast of some of the topics that might arise during small talk. By doing so I have the ability to engage in a wide variety of conversational opening volleys. I try to keep up on current events. I make modest investments of time and attention each week to stay abreast of what's happening in culture, TV, movies, music, and sports.* I maintain a few hobbies, read widely, and of course, I am always ready to talk about the weather.

Then, when the opening volleys of conversations arise — especially with someone I do not know well — I smile, dance in the moment with whatever topic arises, and confidently jump into the conversation at whatever level we have jointly discovered to be possible.

"What Are You Working On?"

Okay, back to networking. Remember networking? This is a book about networking.

We left off at the point where we were trying to find a better way to engage with people. Because my goal is to be helpful, I am trying to

---

* I have become a devotee of podcasts. They are the perfect source of input for times when I am doing other things, like driving, household chores, etc. With a carefully curated smattering of podcast subscriptions, I get just the right dose of relevant information that allows me to engage in a wide range of potential small-talk topics.

quickly reach the point in the conversation where I can tap into who or what I know that might help this person be successful. To do that we have to be talking about something more substantive than the weather.

Our goal, then, is to enjoy the small talk but not linger there. Instead, we want to steer the conversation to a place where we can explore how we might be helpful. As I mentioned above, coming right out and asking, "How can I help you?" or "What do you want to know?" or "To whom may I introduce you?" does not work well. Thankfully, there's a better approach.

Instead of asking, "What do you do?" or "Where are you from?", ask the single most powerful networking question in the world. If you want to get right to the heart of what's important to the person to whom you are talking, ask them, "What are you working on?"[35]

This is, without a doubt, the best networking question of all time. I particularly love the delightful ambiguity that it presents, serving as an invitation to lean in and go somewhere interesting with the conversation. Just as people subconsciously negotiate small talk, in this case they will almost instantly decide whether to answer with something safe and mundane or to venture into something more risky or profound.

I imagine an internal dialogue inside their heads. "What do you mean, 'what am I working on?'… at home?"

Sure, I think to myself. If that's what came to mind for you, tell me what you are working on at home. Perhaps you have just moved to a new house and need help with finding a painter or a handyman. I can recommend a couple. Maybe your kids are applying to colleges or struggling with math. I can help. Yes, what are you working on at home?

In America it is quite common to talk about our professional lives. Sometimes when I ask people what they're working on, their look of intrigue takes them to their jobs. "What do you mean, 'what am I working on?'…at work?"* Yes, definitely, tell me what you are working

---

* In *Part IV — Networking at Work*, we will explore the power of growing and nurturing your network inside of your current organization. Understanding what your colleagues are working on is a powerful asset and a key element of effective collaboration as well as career success.

on at work. Tell me about that project that is challenging you, that colleague who mystifies you, or that customer who exacerbates you. I've worked in dozens of organizations, in several countries, and in various capacities. I might be able to help. If that's what came to mind when I asked, let's talk about what you're working on at work.

Since people often know that I am a leadership and career coach, when I ask people what they're working on, I get that look of hope that says, "What do you mean, 'what am I working on?'... in my career?" Yes, let's talk about your career. How are you stretching yourself? What are you reaching for that you will be ready for in twelve to eighteen months? Careers require care and feeding and attention. You should always be stretching yourself to learn something new and develop new skills. I can help. What are you working on in your career?

Finally, the question, "What are you working on?" can be one of those big, general, all-around questions. "What do you mean, 'what am I working on?'... in life?" Certainly. If you're like me, you're trying to knock off a few pounds, exercise more, get better sleep, be more mindful, spend less time staring at screens, and find a way to fund your golden years. Further, I've got a lot of miles on these tires and all the roads weren't paved. What are you working on in life? I can certainly commiserate, and who knows, I might be able to help.

There are an infinite number of ways a person might respond to the open-ended question, "What are you working on?", beyond the four general categories of home, work, career, and life. However, these categories cover a wide gamut of potential responses that are typical in the context of professional networking. They also provide me with potential follow-up questions if the person fails to appreciate ambiguity with the same delight that I do. If I sense hesitation in the person, I will take the lead and pick a category that seems appropriate based on our small-talk "negotiation." Asking "What are you working on at work?" or "What are you working on in your career?" can open the door to a fruitful conversation that otherwise would have offered little opportunity for either party to explore possible ways to be helpful.

Rack Your Brain

Opening a conversational space with an inviting question such as "What are you working on?" creates an opportunity for you to step into that vulnerable space with them. Seek first to understand. As your understanding of their challenges and aspirations takes shape, begin to query your rich reserves of knowledge and your network for ways in which you might be helpful. While you are listening and conversing, continually run a loop through your head, asking yourself, "Who do I know and what do I know that might help this person be more successful in their endeavors?"

This is the heart of networking: engaging in meaningful conversations while you constantly rack your brain with the questions, "Who do I know and what do I know that might help this person be successful?"

World's Worst Networking Question

"What are you working on?" is such a powerful, relationship-building question because it invites both parties to lean into the conversation. It's personal, inviting people to talk about themselves at whatever level they find comfortable in that moment.

On the other hand, my candidate for the worst networking question is, "What do you do?" It is a vapid, impersonal query that does very little to assist me in my quest to be helpful. "So, you are a doctor (or a project manager, or a VP, or whatever). That's nice."

The problem with asking someone their occupation is that it doesn't produce anything actionable. What do I do with the fact that you are a doctor or a project manager? "What do you do?" is a closed-ended question that offers little room for exploration.

In the end, I don't care what you do. Our jobs do not define us. We all must do something to earn a livelihood, and beyond my fascination with the myriad creative ways that people have found to earn a living, what you do is neither here nor there.

However, as a fellow human being on this often-surreal journey we call life, I care deeply about what you are working on. We work on things that matter to us. And it is in our challenges and aspirations that we find meaning. I want to relate to you—and be helpful if I can—based on what you are working on, not what you do.

A Shift in Intent

Leading with genuine curiosity about what people are working on—and then listening to their answers—is a powerful way to engage the world. It represents a shift in intent from living with an attitude of WIIFM to building and maintaining a web of professional relationships with a spirit of helpfulness and collaboration. I am sure there are more ways to slice the question "What are you working on?", but the broad swaths of home, work, career, and life cover a lot of ground. It is one of the most powerful questions in the world for fostering connections, deepening relationships, enabling collaboration, leveraging your talents, and making the world a better place to work.

Chapter 12

What Are **YOU** Working On?

Nor does anyone light a lamp and put it under a basket, but on the lampstand, and it gives light to all who are in the house.

Matthew 5:15

Until now, our approach to networking has been to honor our intrinsic altruism and engage others with a spirit of helpfulness. We are operating from a position of "paying it forward." Our intent is to see networking not as an occasion to get something for ourselves but as an opportunity to leverage our knowledge, experience, and connections in the service of others. I have urged you to suppress the natural urge to ask, "What's in it for me?" and, instead, to be generous with your offerings of favors, information, and introductions that draw upon your rich web of skills and experiences.

Lest you think that I am advocating that we all become doormats who allow people to take endless advantage of our generosity, rest assured, I am not. As you expand your network with the mindset of being helpful, you will soon find yourself surrounded with like-minded people. Anyone who does not share this mindset of helpfulness should not stay on your radar—or in your network—for very long.

Networking works because of the norm of reciprocity.[36] Imagine yourself in a conversation with a skilled networker in which you have made it past the small talk and have been exploring what the other person is working on. What do you think is the first thing *they* are going to ask *you* when they have the chance? Any skilled networker will come right out and ask, in some form or another, "What are *you* working on?" When emotionally healthy people sense your spirit of helpfulness, they can't help but offer to reciprocate that helpfulness.

The whole system hinges on something of a quirk in the human species. As George Monbiot explains in *Out of the Wreckage*,

> There is something deeply weird about humanity... This phrase does not refer to our skills with language or our use of tools or ability to change our environment, remarkable though these are. It refers to our astonishing degree of altruism: our kindness towards other members of our species. We possess an unparalleled sensitivity to the needs of others, a unique level of concern about their welfare, and a peerless ability to create moral norms that generalize and enforce these tendencies.[37]

Networking is about reciprocity and mutually beneficial relationships. You don't have to worry about getting your fair share. The world is full of generous people. If the people you encounter—or the people already in your network—don't share your spirit of helpfulness, move on until you find people who do. You are building your tribe. There is no place in it for parasites.

Don't Be a Dead Fish

You know how sometimes, when you shake someone's hand, they offer you a limp, wimpy handshake that feels like they have extended a dead fish or a sloppy dish rag? Don't do that. Weak handshakes communicate insecurity or a lack of interest.

Similarly, in the realm of networking don't offer someone a weak response when they ask you what you are working on. I am saddened when I ask someone what they are working on and I get a deer-in-the-headlights look while they fumble for a response. Answers like, "Not much" or "Oh, just keeping busy" give me nothing to work with in my quest to be helpful. It's as if I reached out my hand and they handed me a dead fish. I'm standing there ready to rack my brain with the questions, "Who do I know and what do I know that might be helpful to you?" Everything works better if, when I'm trying to be helpful, you give me something to work with.

Help People Help You

Anticipate gestures of reciprocity. To get the most out of your networking, it is essential that you can articulate the things you are working on in the various dimensions of your life. Networking is a dialogue, a dance. You must show up with your dancing shoes on. Help people help you. Come to the meetings prepared to offer the other person something to work with.

Context Is Everything

Different people can help you in different ways. In real-life situations, your optimal answer to the question, "What Are You Working On?" will vary widely, depending on the person with whom you are speaking and the context in which you find yourself. A few examples might help to illuminate what I mean:

- One of the people in my network is an accomplished baker. Since I recently took inspiration from his success and made my own sourdough starter, with him I am likely to answer that I am working on making the perfect bâtard. While my crusts have been coming out delicious, the rise is tending to be a little flat.

- Many of the people in my network are in the technology and computer worlds. If I meet with one of these IT contacts, I am likely to describe how I am working on refreshing my website with an updated WordPress template and migrating to a new hosting provider. As much as I like to nerd out with website design and CSS, I am in over my head and could use some help.

- If I am attending a conference with fellow coaches, I am likely to say something about how I am working on deepening my listening skills and being less "preachy" with my clients. Listening is hard.

- And if I am meeting with one of my contacts who I know is a devotee of meditation, I am likely to answer that I am working on being more mindful. I grew up in Canada and recently had the opportunity to return to more northern latitudes, albeit still in the United States. I am finding my senses awakened with the deeper rhythms of the northern seasons and would welcome their insights on how to embrace that even further.

All these scenarios suggest topics I could talk about with anyone who might be interested. However, when I prepare to meet with someone, I target my answers to not only have a better chance of being interesting but also, and most important, because I hope to leverage their knowledge and network for a little help. That's how you build mutually beneficial relationships. That's how networking works.

Assume the Best in People

Our goal is not only to engage the world in a spirit of helpfulness but to do so in a way that draws out the best intentions in others as well. I believe that every emotionally healthy person wants to be helpful when they can. Occasionally it simply does not occur to them. Other times they just don't know what to do or where to start. Our approach brings the spirit to light and makes the helpfulness inviting and contagious.

We start with the simple assumption that the other person does, indeed, have good intentions. Beginning with the assumption that people want to be helpful can go a long way toward getting on the same wavelength with them.

Next, anticipate that at some point in the conversation, the other person is going to ask what *you* are working on. The key here is to realize that the question may not be phrased in exactly that way. Not everyone has read this book or attended one of my workshops, so most times the question will not be worded so plainly. Sometimes inexperienced networkers will ask seemingly benign questions like, "What do you do?" or "What's up?"

Since I am assuming that the person wants to be helpful, I ignore the fact that I consider such questions to be vacuous in networking situations. Instead, I subtly lead them into my mindset for networking. I assume they are interested in what I am working on, even if it never occurs to them to ask me directly. Regardless of how they initiate the networking conversation, I briefly answer their question and then proceed to tell them something from my life that I am working on that I think they might find relevant. The conversations often go something like this:

> Networker: "Heather, what do you do?"
>
> Me: "I'm a leadership coach and I've been doing a lot of work lately on team culture and interpersonal dynamics. I think I have figured out the root cause of dysfunction and politics in organizations. I am hoping to connect with people who want to optimize their team environments."

Or perhaps, if I'm talking to a computer whiz,

> Networker: "So, what brings you here?"
>
> Me: "I'm a career coach, but lately I have been working on getting a new template installed on my website so that it adapts properly to mobile screens. I've learned more about WordPress and CSS than I ever thought I would want to know."

To the extent that you know something about the other person, you want to customize and contextualize your response. As the person hears about a challenge you are facing or listens to the details of how you're striving to grow, stretch, or improve some aspect of your life, it is almost impossible for them to *not* try to think of some way to be helpful. It's as if humans automatically go into altruistic problem-solving mode when presented with a challenge. You can shape the conversation — and the person's thinking — simply through your assumptions and the way that you frame your response.

Of course, there will always be people in the world who are interested only in getting something for themselves without understanding the art of building mutually beneficial relationships. I call these people "net-grovelers." They will not pick up on your subtle cues and they will not be interested in being helpful. Identify such people as quickly as possible and walk away. You do not want or need these kinds of people in your network.

It's a good time to point out that guiding conversations in this way is not for everyday encounters. These guidelines are for networking contexts in which both parties are actively looking for ways to create or strengthen a networking connection. While I am always keen to be helpful, I do not redirect every small-talk query toward something I am working on.

Be Prepared

When it comes to networking and building relationships, the more you know about a person, the greater the potential to strengthen that relationship. A little insight increases the odds that you will be able to exchange favors and information.

This is obvious, really. The more you know about a person, the easier it is to identify what the two of you have in common. By doing a bit of homework in advance, you will know some of their values and what's important to them. You will have a sense of who they know and the circles in which they run. You may be able to glean where they work and what they do. Not only do these insights enable you to quickly tap into who and what you know that might be helpful to the other person, but you will also align more quickly with them, making it easier for the other person to reciprocate.

I can't stress this enough. Most people want to be helpful. Most people, however, have no idea how to do so. Your thoughtfulness in advance, along with a bit of reconnaissance, will help you be of assistance and will help them help you.

Getting to Know Someone

Except for public figures, it used to be difficult to get to know someone without meeting them. When I started my career, the only way to learn about someone was in person or through a friend. The internet has changed everything. The way we share our lives online and through social media means there are now countless ways to begin to get to know someone before you meet face-to-face.

Start with LinkedIn, the database of record for the modern career. An astute reader perusing a well-constructed LinkedIn profile will find a trove of information and potential insights. Where do they work? Where did they go to school? What are some of their interests? Beyond their career history, I can usually get a good sense of many other aspects of their personality as well. We'll go into much more detail in Chapter 18 on what we can glean, infer, and discern from a well-constructed LinkedIn profile.

Beyond LinkedIn, take a moment to do a quick Google search and see what comes up.

- Do they have a Twitter account? This will give you insights into the more informal side of their personality.

- Are they on Facebook? Look at the more personal things that they deem important.

- Do they have a blog or other writing on the internet? Read (or at least skim) what they have written.

It is more than worthwhile to avail yourself of publicly available information as you prepare to meet with someone. By doing so, you can start your conversation at a much deeper level and progress more rapidly toward a mutually beneficial relationship.

By doing some reconnaissance before you meet, you will not only be able to ask better questions and more quickly find ways to be helpful, but you will also be able to sculpt your answer when someone asks, "What are *you* working on?" in a way that will make it easier for them to be helpful to you. This is the essence of a great networking mindset.

Exercise: What You Are Working On

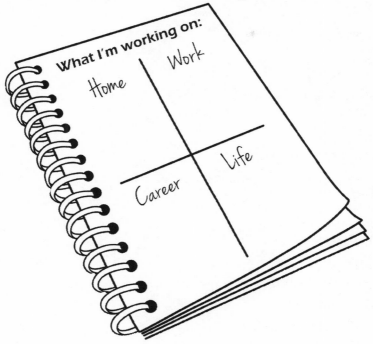

Despite the highly contextual nature of what you might share in networking conversations, it's important to have a baseline from which to start. Set aside some time to sketch out the general areas in your life in which you invest time, energy, and thought. This will enable you to have a well-conceived answer when asked, "What are you working on" in just about any context.*

Spend a few moments right now and consider what you are working on in each of our four general categories. Start with a blank sheet of paper and draw two lines down the middle—one vertical, one horizontal—to divide the page into four quadrants. Give yourself five to ten minutes for each quadrant. What are you working on at home? At work? In your career? In life?

---

* All of the exercises in this book are included in *The Workbook of Helpful Exercises*, which can be downloaded at **heatherhollick.com/helpful**.

1. What are you working on at home?

What is going on in your personal life? What are some of the challenges, projects, and activities that occupy you when you are at home?

2. What are you working on at work?

What projects are you working on? What are some of your team and corporate goals?

3. What are you working on in your career?

What are some of your professional goals and ambitions? To what do you aspire?

4. What are you working on in life?

What are some of your personal goals and ambitions for the next five years? For the rest of your life?

Chapter 13

Follow Up

Whatever you do
Do with your might
For a job done by half
Is never done right.

Mom

Meeting people and engaging in meaningful conversations is only a small portion of the totality of networking. Just as a network is not a roster of people but the *links between* people, the real power of networking emerges not during the times when you meet with someone but during the *times and spaces between* your rendezvous.

Recall that networking is about *creating, freshening,* and *strengthening* links between you and other people. While meeting people face-to-face is a great way to create and freshen links, strengthening those connections takes follow-through, intention, and effort. Follow-through starts with follow-up.

Capture Notes and Highlights

As my dad used to say, I have a great memory—it's just short. It seems that the more time that goes by the more I forget. As a result, within twenty-four hours of meeting with someone, I capture the highlights from that meeting. Depending on how well I know the person, I will either make a few updates in the "Notes" field of my address book entry for them or create a note in Evernote. I capture such things as

- Relevant names: spouse, children, boss, colleagues, pets;

- Relevant dates: birthdays, anniversaries, upcoming milestones in their lives;
- Any additions to their background or backstory that I didn't already know;
- Major themes of our conversation;
- How I met them (if this is not the first time we have met);
- What they are working on.

Pass On Relevant Information

One of the loops running through our heads when we are networking is, "*What* do I know that could help this person be successful?" As part of your follow-up, act on this knowledge. Pass on links, articles, information, and resources that you think could be helpful. It's especially important to provide links for any of the resources you mentioned in your conversation. How many times have you come home from meeting with someone and searched in vain for the name of a book or TED Talk that they were raving about? What a treat it is to get an email with the links to all the resources that you discussed.

Make Introductions

The other loop running through our minds when we are networking is, "*Who* do I know that could help this person?" Introductions are the bedrock of networking. Connecting two people who go on to have a mutually beneficial relationship is a powerful and rewarding deed. They will both be grateful to you for the introduction—thus strengthening both connections for you.

If you happen to be at an event in which the two people you want to introduce are in the room, then don't hesitate. Facilitate an introduction in the moment. Most of the time, however, the other party to the introduction will be elsewhere and the introduction will come later. There are good ways—and some not-so-good ways—to make these introductions.

Email is your primary tool here. Extraverts will be tempted to pick up the phone, but stay with me on this. Email allows you to send background information and links to the other person's LinkedIn profile, giving both parties the opportunity to "do their homework" before they connect for the first time.

It's best to prepare the soil first, to facilitate a successful introduction. Resist the temptation to jot off an email to both people saying, "Jane, meet John; John, meet Jane." I have received a number of these well-meaning introductions from well-intentioned people, but the introductions have rarely led to meaningful network connections for me.

Even if you provide a few sentences of background and introductory insights, you put both people on the spot. People lead busy, complicated lives. The timing of a good introduction needs to be right, and both people need to be ready to be connected. Connecting two people who are not ready to be connected — or worse, really aren't a good match — is a waste of everyone's time. Further, it does nothing to enhance the quality of your network. In some cases, it may even diminish you in the eyes of one or both people.

Instead, send separate emails to both people whom you want to introduce. Let's suppose that you and I just met, and I believe that you should connect with my friend Isabelle. The first thing that I will do when I get home is compose an email *back to you* reminding you that I think you should connect with Isabelle. I will include a few comments on why I think it would be good for you two to connect and a link to Isabelle's LinkedIn profile. I'll close my email with the magic phrase, "*If and when* you are ready to connect, I am happy to make an introduction."

This last sentence is the most important in the entire email. An introduction is an invitation for two people to begin a relationship. Don't take it lightly. The worst is when, out of the blue, some well-meaning soul in my network sends an introductory email and copies both of us on the same message. Now we are both on the spot. We like you, respect you, and appreciate the gesture. But, for any number of reasons, now may not be the ideal time to make this introduction.

Timing is everything. The best introductions are not only between the right people but also *at the right time*. While I may have an inkling that you and Isabelle should meet, I have no way of knowing whether now is the right time. Only you and Isabelle know that. I will not be offended or disappointed if you never take me up on the offer for the introduction.

If you do decide to meet Isabelle, you now have the space to do your homework before connecting with her. You will check out her LinkedIn profile and digest what else you can find from her presence on the web, before setting out to make a network connection.

Finally, the email that I send you will be constructed so that, when you are ready, you can forward it to Isabelle if you would like. This helps complete the warm introduction and offers some credibility when Isabelle receives your first email.

Next, after my email to you, I'll send an email to Isabelle as well, touting your strengths. I will go on to explain why I think it would be good for the two of you to connect, and that you may be reaching out to her soon. Of course, I will include a link to your LinkedIn profile so that Isabelle can do her homework as well.

Having made both introductions separately, I have done several things:

- I have piqued both of your curiosities on why you might want to meet each other.

- I have given both you and Isabelle enough background and information (i.e., LinkedIn profiles) to get an idea of the person you are going to meet *before you actually meet!* This will give both of you the opportunity to do a bit of preparation, making it likely that your eventual connection will be stronger and more productive.

- If either of you decides that it's not a good match or the timing isn't right, nothing is lost. No harm, no foul.

Good follow-up is an art. Keep on following up whenever you come across people or information that makes you think of that person. It can be days, weeks, or months later; there is no statute of limitations on sharing information. This is the essence of the networking mindset and a vital aspect of keeping the links in your network fresh.

Further, an email out of the blue with an introduction or a link to a relevant article is a powerful way to freshen a connection. It may not only be helpful, but it also brings you top of mind for them, lets them know you are thinking of them, and reminds them that they are an active part of your network.

Chapter 14

Rounding Out
the Mindset

It's not only moving that creates new starting points.
Sometimes, all it takes is a subtle shift in perspective, an
opening of the mind, an intentional pause and reset, or a new
route to start to see new options and new possibilities.

Kristin Armstrong, Olympic Gold-Medal Cyclist[38]

In the next two chapters we will delve into more detail on how to guide a conversation beyond small talk so that both parties can comfortably explore ways to strengthen their connection and be helpful to one another. Before we do that, let's explore a few additional considerations about the networking mindset.

Future Connections

Sometimes — indeed, most of the time — when you interact with someone, you will feel like you are drawing a blank. As much as you embrace a spirit of helpfulness, you won't be able to think of a person or a piece of information to share in the moment. Not to worry. The opportunity to share often comes later. Listen, inquire, and learn as much as you can about the person. Absorb their answers and file the information away for future reference.

Most of the time your ability to be helpful won't emerge until some point in the future. Perhaps you haven't yet connected with the person to whom you need to introduce the person in front of you. Or perhaps the information that you need to share won't come to mind or cross your path until days, weeks, or months later. In the meantime, just keep asking questions, listening, and conversing. The more you know and understand about the person you are talking to, the more likely you can exchange a favor or information.

Thinking not just in the moment but for future possibilities infuses your networking with a spirit of anticipation. This is the heart of networking. It's not an activity. Networking is a mindset. It's a way of thinking about your world and engaging the people in it. As you read articles and think about who you might send them to, that is networking. As you look through your LinkedIn connections and consider which of these people you should introduce to one another, that's networking.

Strength in Diversity

When you think of your network as a medium to exchange favors and information, you quickly realize that the more diversity you have in your network, the greater the likelihood that you will be able to make connections and introductions. You never know who you will meet, what they might be working on, or what problems they might be trying to solve. The more diversity the better.

- **Geography**: Reach for broad geographic diversity in your network. Because I have worked primarily in North America, the bulk of my network comprises people from across the US and Canada. However, I am inspired by the fact that I am also connected to people from as far away as Scotland, Hong Kong, Japan, and Argentina.

- **Expertise and Profession**: Network with people from a broad range of industries and expertise. While it's important to be well connected in *your* industry, reach beyond your profession to connect with people who earn a living in any number of ways. From schoolteachers to firefighters, from business leaders to actors, mix it up.

- **Interests**: People who share your interests tend to think like you do. While this can seem invigorating in the short run, it's stifling when it comes to networking. The more varied the interests are of the people you know, the more likely you are to have access to unexpected information, and the more likely you are to introduce two people in your network.

- **Diversity of Thought**: Connect with people who think and process information differently than you do. For example, accountants and musicians approach problems very differently. So do engineers and medical doctors. Seek to have a wide array of thinkers in your network.

- **Cultures**: Seek to incorporate into your network people raised in different cultures. People from different cultures often understand the world very differently, offering fresh and diverse perspectives on things you may have taken for granted your entire life.

- **Socioeconomic Status**: This is a tough one. We are drawn to — and are comfortable — with people in our own socioeconomic class. Fight this tendency. People are people. Seek to connect with people both above and below your current socioeconomic status.

- **Age**: The most robust networks represent multiple generations. I am fortunate to have people in my network with ages ranging from their late teens to their late eighties. Each decade represented in my network offers a different perspective, a different set of life experiences, and a different network that I can connect with mine.

Treat It Like an Asset

Your network is an asset. Furthermore, your network is an asset that is owned wholly by you. It is part of who you are. While many of your current network connections may work for the same employer that you do, your employer does not own your network. Your network transcends your job and your company. It's a key aspect of your identity and a valuable resource that you build and carry with you throughout your career. You bring it with you to your company, and you always have it available to share with your community. No outside force—no employer, no twist of fate—can take it away from you.

The only thing that can diminish your network is negligence. The older we get and the more established we become in our careers, the faster the months and years seem to fly by. Do not take your network for granted. Lack of care and feeding results in network connections that fade and a network that loses potency. It's up to you to build your network the way you want it, and it falls wholly to you to nurture and maintain it.

Be Fearless

Networking anchored in a spirit of helpfulness changes the game. It shifts the focus of networking and professional relationships from "What's in it for me?" to "How can I be helpful?" This represents a profound inner shift from egocentricity to an acknowledgment that we are all interconnected. It has broad cultural and economic implications as well.

I used to be afraid of networking. Unsteady in my inexperience, I would stumble over my social awkwardness. I was often paralyzed by the fear that people would reject me. My fears were not unfounded. People *had* rejected me. Or, more precisely, they had rejected *me*!

But they can't reject me anymore, not because I have become impervious to rejection but because I put myself out there differently now. Instead of engaging in networking with a vague sense of trying to get something, I started engaging the world with an offer to be helpful. Rather than WIIFM, I ask myself, "Who do I know and what do I know that could help this person be successful?" When presented with an offer to be helpful, people can either accept it or reject it. No worries if they don't want or can't use my help. I am neither offended nor discouraged.

In this sense, networking is not like dating. I'm not putting *myself* out there to be accepted or rejected. I am extending an offer to be helpful. I am offering to leverage who and what I know to help someone and maybe, just maybe, make the world a better place to live and work. They're welcome to reject my offer to help, but they can't reject me.

Take the Call

You now have everything you need to build and maintain a powerful network. You have a clear sense of what a network is, so much so that you can visualize the freshness and strength of each link between yourself and everyone you know. You understand that networking is not about going to events but about finding ways that work *for you* to create, freshen, and strengthen those links. You understand how small talk paves the way to the most powerful networking question of all, and you now have a permanent loop in your brain that asks, "Who do I know and what do I know that could help this person be successful?" And finally, you have learned how to help your network help you, by thinking in advance about how to describe what, in fact, you are working on.

All that remains is for you to turn your sights outward, where your network is waiting for you.

Maintain an Air of Expectation

My approach to networking is to engage the world with a spirit of helpfulness and a "pay-it-forward" attitude. One of the exciting things about this mindset is that you are constantly and pleasantly surprised. You never know when an introduction will come your way or a truly fascinating person will cross your path.

The key is to maintain an air of anticipation, a sense of expectation that you are about to meet someone interesting. Vibrant networks are constantly exchanging favors and passing along information. However, you must show up and pay attention if you want to be part of that exchange.

This means that when you get inquiries from your network, you should respond quickly. Return calls and emails. Even a polite "I am swamped right now, but I wanted you to know that I got your message" is better than no response at all. I am talking, here, only about

people you consider to be in your network. Cold calls, unknown recruiters who may be trolling LinkedIn, and non-personalized invitations to connect on LinkedIn are excepted.

Similarly, close the loop on introductions. Be generous. Offer to
meet with the person being introduced to you, or connect with them
through a phone call.

Trust your network. This is your tribe. It is the people to whom you
are loyal and who, you can assume, are loyal to you. They won't take
advantage of you, and the rewards far outweigh the risks.

Part III
Networking In Action

Chapter 15

The Case for LinkedIn

If you don't know where you are going, you'll end up someplace else.

Yogi Berra

We are now going to look at how our new networking mindset might transform such things as how we use social media, how we work a room at an event, the role of networking when looking for a job, and how to make informational interviews a key tool in your networking toolbox.

Let me begin by sharing the encounter that opened my eyes to the power of preparing for meetings. Several years ago, I met a gentleman I'll call Chuck at a networking event for technology executives. With mutual interests and similar backgrounds, we hit it off. Within a few minutes it was clear that we needed to continue the conversation over a cup of coffee. Plans were made.

Just prior to our coffee meeting, I took a few minutes to study Chuck's LinkedIn profile. He had rich detail about the places he had worked and the impact he had made. In minutes, I had a good picture of what he had accomplished in his career to date, his leadership style, and a general sense of what was important to him.

When we finally sat down at the coffee shop, it was instantly clear that he had similarly reviewed my LinkedIn profile. Within minutes we were conversing at a level that surprised both of us. We were talking about our philosophies of leadership, our belief in teams, our challenges in driving change, and our deep desire to make a difference. It was as if we were two old friends who had known each other for years—except we had barely just met. Because we both had a wealth of information on our LinkedIn profiles and because we had both done our homework, our conversation started off at a level much deeper than you'd expect from two people meeting at length for the first time. This is the value of a pair of good LinkedIn profiles.

Social media has revolutionized our ability to stay in touch in a geographically distributed world. LinkedIn, Twitter — and to some degree, Facebook — have made it possible to build and maintain a rich web of professional relationships with people from around the globe. Of course, there are many more social networking tools than LinkedIn, Twitter, and Facebook. For our purposes, however, we will focus on LinkedIn and Twitter. These platforms are familiar to most professionals and appear to be the most useful and powerful tools to create, freshen, and strengthen links. You can generalize the ideas to Facebook, Google+, Pinterest, WhatsApp, and whatever other online social outlet you use to connect with other people.

What Is LinkedIn?

Launched in the spring of 2003 with a mission to connect the world's professionals, LinkedIn has been on a slow and steady growth trajectory ever since. Over the years, the company has gone public, made several acquisitions, began publishing articles from "influencers," and reached into the online and corporate training arenas through the acquisition of Lynda.com. Further, Microsoft's acquisition of LinkedIn in 2016 adds a shadow of uncertainty as to the future direction and usefulness of the platform.

I don't know where LinkedIn is going as a company or as a platform, but I do know they have a good reputation and some decent privacy settings. By selecting some of their best features and leveraging them with surgical precision, you can make LinkedIn a valuable tool for building and maintaining a network of professional relationships in our geographically dispersed world.

Regardless of how you feel about the corporate side of LinkedIn, it has grown to be the gravitational center of the online professional networking universe. As of 2017 the platform represents more than

530 million professional profiles from more than 200 countries.[39] There are many different reasons why people use LinkedIn, and no shortage of books, articles, and resources espousing how to use it for these reasons (just do a quick search on Amazon for "LinkedIn"). Our interest is to explore the use of LinkedIn as *a tool that enhances and amplifies our ability to network.* As we have already discussed, LinkedIn is well suited as a place to post job opportunities and find talent. In the hands of a savvy networker, it can be much more than that.

Eight Ways LinkedIn Helps You Network

In this chapter we will look at the role that LinkedIn can play in networking as well as the reasons you might want a complete and robust LinkedIn profile. In the next chapter we'll dig into the essentials of your profile and the mechanics of creating it and keeping it up to date so that it represents you well and serves as a useful resource for everyone in your network. Before we dig into the "how" of being on LinkedIn, let's explore the "why." Here are eight overlapping and complementary ways to use LinkedIn as part of your overall networking activity.

1. Declare Yourself

First and foremost, LinkedIn is the database of record for your career. It is your online résumé and so much more. Your profile reflects your past as well as your aspirations. It proclaims who you are as a professional, spanning your career objectives, work history, college experience, favorite hobbies, and much more. It is the first stop for recruiters and the de facto starting point for anyone who wants to know anything about your career.

2. Enhance Introductions

As I mentioned in Chapter 14, LinkedIn profiles play a key role in facilitating email introductions. Your complete LinkedIn profile helps others help you. Here's what I mean: imagine that I set out to introduce you to someone in my network named Bob.

As in my example above about making an introduction with Isabelle, the first thing I will do is compose an email to Bob with a few comments about why I think the two of you should connect. I will be generous with my impressions of you and do my best to jump-start a mutually beneficial relationship. Most important, I will embed a link to your LinkedIn profile, so that Bob can check you out for himself.

When Bob receives my email introduction of you, he will inevitably click the link to your LinkedIn profile. His eyes will immediately be drawn to your photo, where he will make a visual connection with you. Then he'll read your title and your summary to see how you proclaim yourself to the world.

Next, he'll scan your work history and scroll down to see where you went to school. In about ninety seconds he will take in a wealth of information about you. If you have any recommendations, he may explore what they say about you, paying particular attention to how others describe you. If you and Bob share mutual connections, he will explore them and ponder the significance of the intersection.

He may click on your "Contact Information" tab, where he'll look for a link to your Twitter account and any other online sites that you would like him to know about. As you can see, it is easy to spend anywhere from a few minutes to several hours exploring your history, your career, and whatever tangents your profile may have sent him on.

Based on my recommendation and the rich background of your profile, Bob will begin to formulate in his mind whether and how he might be helpful to you. The more information in your profile, the more Bob has to work with, and the greater the likelihood that he will think of a way to be helpful to you. If, on the other hand, you have a weak profile, a lousy picture (or, God forbid, no photo), my introduction will not have nearly the impact that a complete profile with a good picture will.

Sure, before LinkedIn, an introduction from a mutual connection would have been enough to facilitate a connection between two people. But we're living in the era of social media, and your LinkedIn profile takes the introduction to a whole different level. All of the information in your profile helps people feel connected to you before they even meet you. How cool is that?

3. Refresh Your Memory

But wait, there's more. The power of LinkedIn extends far beyond facilitating introductions. As we continue to build our case for using LinkedIn, recall that the essence of networking is freshening and strengthening the links between you and the people in your network. LinkedIn can play a key role in the freshening department. With a quick glance at your profile, I can refresh my memory on anything related to your career: where you went to school, your current employer, and what you've been doing since the last time we got together.

Granted, skimming someone's LinkedIn profile is a passive endeavor — not nearly as invigorating as freshening a connection with a face-to-face meeting. However, even in this passive activity I am constantly asking myself, "Who do I know that might help this person be successful?" The more information I can keep top of mind about the people in my network, the more likely I can be helpful. This, in turn, makes it more likely that I can forge powerful connections with people. LinkedIn helps me keep up to date and remember key facts about the people in my network.

4. Prepare for Meetings

LinkedIn plays an invaluable role in helping you to prepare to meet with people. For people with a keen eye and a knack for induction, a well-constructed LinkedIn profile offers a wealth of information and potential insights about someone with whom you want to strengthen a relationship. Most LinkedIn profiles will reveal

- How they see themselves and who they aspire to be (the "Summary" section);
- The major milestones of their professional life (the "Career History" section);

- Their interests (the jobs they have held, the groups to which they belong, the organizations for which they have volunteered);
- Key attributes of their leadership style and personal preferences (gleaned both from the way they talk about their accomplishments and from the way that others describe them in recommendations);
- Where they currently live (stated right under their name at the top of their profile);
- Where they have lived (gleaned from where they went to college and sometimes from job descriptions);
- Their current interests and how their interests and talents have evolved over their career (start with their college majors; then read their "Experience" section from bottom to top);
- The connections you have in common.

In addition to the explicit information in a person's LinkedIn profile, I make a best guess at several other characteristics that might help me understand and connect with them at a deeper level more quickly when we meet. Here are a few additional items that I infer and surmise while looking at someone's LinkedIn profile:

- Their age to the nearest decade. We have very different priorities and evolving values in our twenties, thirties, forties, and so on (most people list the years they attended college. It is reasonable to guess that they graduated from undergraduate education in their early twenties);
- Whether their preferences tend toward introversion or extraversion (I can often make a good guess from their photo and the way they describe themselves);
- Whether they take in information intuitively or leverage data and their senses (this is the Sensing-Intuition dichotomy on the Myers-Briggs profile);

- Whether they make decisions based on harmony and relationships or on logic and analysis (the Feeling-Thinking dichotomy on the Myers-Briggs profile);
- Whether they prefer action or information-gathering (the Perceiving-Judging dichotomy on the Myers-Briggs profile).

All this, just from spending a few minutes looking at their LinkedIn profile.

It is a tremendous boost for both parties to take advantage of publicly available information as you prepare to meet with someone. It doesn't matter if your best guesses are off. If you are wrong, you will immediately correct and adjust as you get to know each other.

LinkedIn affords you the opportunity to do some thoughtful preparation before you meet someone. It helps you to ask better questions; connect more quickly with a favor, introduction, or information that might be helpful; and better anticipate a question about what *you* are working on. These strike me as invaluable reasons to use LinkedIn.

5. Find Companies That Are Hiring

LinkedIn has all but cornered the market on "talent solutions."[40] It has become the go-to place for job postings and information about companies that are hiring. They even have a dedicated job-searching phone app. When you search for job postings from the dedicated "Jobs" tab on the website, you can immediately see the connections you have in the company.

Matching talented people with job opportunities might even be LinkedIn's sweet spot. The first rule of career progression is: if you're looking for an opportunity, you're looking for a person. Because people on LinkedIn list the companies they work for, LinkedIn might bring opportunities and people together better than any other service available right now.

We'll dig deeper into LinkedIn's role in a job search in Chapter 20, which is dedicated to learning how to use networking in your search for the next career opportunity. For now, suffice it to say that LinkedIn is a goldmine of information about jobs and career opportunities.

6. Provide Links to Other Websites

Most people have multiple footprints scattered across the internet. Many have Twitter accounts, Facebook pages, Instagram accounts, company websites, personal blogs, passion projects, and volunteer activities, to name a few. The problem is, once I have found you, how can I find the other sites and accounts that you want me to know about?

LinkedIn's contact panel to the rescue. You can link your Twitter account and store links for up to three of your other sites and accounts. They show up at the top of your profile under the "Contact" tab.*

LinkedIn is the first place I look when I am trying to find someone on the web. The contact section of your profile is your electronic business card. Populate it wisely.

7. Keep Track of Who's In Your Network

At its core, LinkedIn is a database. As such, it can be a useful tool in your networking toolbox. I use LinkedIn as an online reflection of the active connections I maintain with people in real life. In addition to listing the names of everyone in my network, LinkedIn, by offering basic contact information, provides an email address, a phone number (if you've included one in your profile), your birthday (if you've made it available to your network connections), and the date that we connected. While I regularly plead with LinkedIn to provide richer contact relationship management (CRM) functionality, this basic information, accompanied by the depth and breadth of a profile, makes it an indispensable networking tool.

8. Engage In Groups and Discussions

Finally, on the list of reasons why LinkedIn is useful, we have the platform's groups and discussions. They are one of the site's most popular and endearing features. There are hundreds of thousands of groups on

---

* Unfortunately, there is no dedicated place to link to your Facebook account in the same way that LinkedIn connects your Twitter account. If you use Facebook and want it referenced from your LinkedIn profile, add your Facebook URL as one of your three other websites.

countless topics. If you can't find a group that suits your purpose, start one of your own. It only takes a few minutes.

As with most things on the internet, my experience with groups and discussions on LinkedIn is mixed. While I have a few that are invaluable resources, they tend to be noisy places populated by a few active participants and a small minority of people hell-bent on self-promotion. My advice is to join one or two and get involved in the discussions. You might engage in a few interesting conversations and connect with a few interesting people. Beyond that, their value is limited as a networking tool.

Up Next

If LinkedIn didn't exist, I am confident that someone would create it. In this chapter I've outlined eight reasons why it is a valuable, if not indispensable, tool in your networking and career toolbox (although I am admittedly ambivalent on the usefulness of groups). If you don't have a LinkedIn profile, I recommend that you consider creating one. If you already have a profile, I recommend that you read on. Over the next two chapters we will explore how to optimize your profile with networking in mind and then how to use LinkedIn as an integral part of your overall networking activity.

Exercise: LinkedIn Profile Reviews

Train yourself to quickly glean information from people's LinkedIn profiles. These insights are invaluable as you prepare for meetings, irrespective of whether you know the person well, or are meeting them for the first time.*

Step 1. Study the profiles of three to five people you know well.

Given that you know these people well, notice how their profile reflects the things you know about them.

- Look at their profile photo. What do you see and how does it reflect their personality?
- Do they lean toward a preference for introversion or extraversion? What do you see in their profile that reflects that preference?
- How do they describe themselves in the summary and the job descriptions?
- How do other people describe them in the recommendations?
- What are the major milestones in their professional life?
- What are some of their interests?
- What kind of leader are they? How does their profile reflect this?What connections do you have in common?
- Given what you see on their LinkedIn profile, what questions would you want to ask if you were meeting them for the first time?

---

* All of the exercises in this book are included in *The Workbook of Helpful Exercises*, which can be downloaded at **heatherhollick.com/helpful**.

Step 2. Now look up the profiles of three to five people you do not know at all.

Ask yourself variations of the same questions noted above, this time using your best guess based on what you can glean from their profile.

- Look at their profile photo. What do you see and how might it reflect their personality?
- Do you think that they lean toward a preference for introversion or extraversion?
- How do they describe themselves in the summary and the job descriptions?
- How do other people describe them in the recommendations?
- What are the major milestones in their professional life?
- What are some of their interests?
- What kind of leader would you make them out to be?
- What connections do you have in common?
- Given what you see on their LinkedIn profile, what questions would you want to ask if you were meeting that person for the first time?

Chapter 16

Elements of a Great Profile

It ain't bragging if you can do it!

Dizzy Dean

What makes for a great LinkedIn profile? Now that we know how we intend to use LinkedIn, we can talk about what we need in our profile to make it useful both to ourselves and to others in our network.

Before we delve into a few general guidelines, and a tried-and-true method for creating a great profile, note that almost all of my recommendations for your LinkedIn profile also apply to your résumé. Your LinkedIn profile is just a version of your résumé expanded and enhanced by the functionality of an online platform.

The next two chapters are not unlike a recipe for cooking a great meal: ingredients plus directions. In this chapter I'll list the ingredients that go into a profile optimized for networking. In the next chapter I'll outline the directions for combining and blending those ingredients into a great profile.

Current Profile

It's simply not possible for each of us to meet face-to-face, or even exchange emails, with every person in our networks on a regular basis. It *is* possible, however, to periodically check each other's LinkedIn profiles. Granted, visiting someone's profile is a passive, asynchronous interaction, but spending a few moments with a profile allows us to refresh our memories and see what's new. This makes having a current

LinkedIn profile a key element in keeping your network relationships fresh. Honor people's time and intentions when they visit you on LinkedIn by keeping the following sections current:

- Current Title. LinkedIn calls this field your "Headline." That sounds about right. Your headline should reflect who you are as a professional. It doesn't necessarily have to be your current title or be tied to an employer or position. At no time should you list your title as "In Transition" or "Available." Such terms sound desperate. If you can't pin down a good title, then use the "Headline" field to describe how you help people.

- Current Location. Indicate the general area where you are based. Be as general or as specific as you would like. If, like me, you tend to be a bit nomadic, then write what you consider to be your current base of operations.

- Current Contact Information. Your contact information — email, phone number, and relevant websites — is always available to your first-degree connections. Make sure that your profile is up to date with your latest information so that people can get in touch with you wherever you may be in the world.

- Current Summary. Your "Summary" section should reflect your current capabilities and aspirations. This section is where you summarize the highlights of your career so far. It is also the section where you share what you stand for and what you are ready to do next. More on that in the next chapter when we explore the "Three Pass Method" for updating your profile.

- Current Experience. Of course, this section should contain your current work and volunteer positions. You can have multiple current positions, and volunteer positions count. We'll cover this in detail in the next chapter as well.

Complete Profile

After a current profile, the second element for a great LinkedIn profile is a *complete* profile. While a current profile helps keep your network connections fresh, a *complete* profile is a key component of building and maintaining the *strength* of your connections.

While not the story of your entire life, a complete profile includes:

- Your name, title, and company (or industry);
- Your phone number, email address, and a mailing address;*
- A personalized URL;
- A profile photo;
- A summary of your experience, aspirations, and what you've learned;
- Your current and past work and volunteer positions;
- Your education, including the years that you attended;†
- Certifications;
- Publications;
- Interests and hobbies;
- The groups to which you belong;
- A few recommendations received;
- A few recommendations given.

---

* Yes, a mailing address, assuming that you have a business address or PO Box that you feel comfortable sharing with those in your network. In a world where almost all communications are now electronic, sending gifts, cards, thank-you notes, and letters is an ever more powerful way to communicate. Make it easy for your contacts to reach you by including a mailing address in your profile. This information is only visible to your first-degree connections.

† Some people are reluctant to include the years they attended schools for fear that it gives away their age. It does. But with age comes experience, and from experience comes wisdom. Wisdom is invaluable. I love the adage, "Knowledge knows the rules, wisdom knows the exceptions." If you have the wisdom, wear it proudly.

Your Profile Photo

You must have a photo on your profile. Let me say that another way: in the age of social media, not having a photo is not an option. There is something magical about seeing someone's eyes and face, even when it's just a static picture.

I spend a good portion of my business life on the phone, in conference and coaching calls. I will frequently pull up your LinkedIn profile photo and leave it on my screen while we talk. Doing so helps me feel more connected to you. That's the power of a tiny picture.

Seth Godin has written a brilliant article that outlines nine great guidelines for any profile photo that you use for social media. They couldn't be more relevant for your LinkedIn profile. It's so good that I asked Seth if I could reproduce it here in its entirety. He said yes! [41]

> If it's important enough for you to spend your time finding and connecting with new people online, it's important enough to get the first impression right.
>
> If you use any online social network tool, the single most important first impression you make is with the 3600 to 5000 pixels you get for your tiny picture.
>
> In the social group I run, part of my job is to pick the featured members. As a result, I spend a lot of time looking at little pictures. Here's one person's take on the things you can do to avoid wrecking that first impression:
>
> 1. Have a professional or a dedicated amateur take your picture.
>
> 2. Use a white background, or at least a neutral one. No trees! No snowstorms!
>
> 3. The idea of having your significant other in the picture is a good one, at least in terms of maintaining peace in the presence of a jealous or nervous spouse. But the thing is, I'm not friending

your girlfriend, I'm friending you. I'd vote for the picture to be solo.

4. *If you are wearing a hat, you better have both a good reason and a good hat.*

5. *I totally understand that you are shy, modest, and self-effacing. But sabotaging your photo is not a good way to communicate that. We just assume you're a dork.*

6. *Conceptual photos (your foot, a monkey wearing glasses) may give us insight into the real you, but perhaps you could save that insight for the second impression.*

7. *How beautiful you are is a distant second to how happy you are. In my experience, photos that communicate openness and enthusiasm are far more appealing than photos that make you look like a supermodel.*

8. *Cropping is so important. A well-cropped photo sends a huge, subliminal message to other people. If you don't know how to do this, browse through the work of professionals, and see how they do it. It matters.*

9. *Some people have started adding words or signs to their images. If your goal is to communicate that you are the website or you are the company, then this is very smart. If not, then remember the cocktail party rule: if you wouldn't wear it there, don't wear it here.*

10. *If, after reading this list, you don't like your picture, go change it. No reason not to.*

Your profile is often my first—or lingering—impression of you. It's important to get that impression right.

Lose the Letters After Your Name

Avoid the temptation to include your abbreviated credentials as part of your name. I cringe whenever I see the likes of MBA, SPHR, PMP, ACC, CPCC, or CSP emblazoned across the top of someone's profile. With the possible exception of MD or PhD, a string of capital letters after your name screams insecurity.

Make it clear in the rest of your profile that you have various degrees and credentials. The people who want and need to know that information will discover it and, in their discovery, appreciate the value of the credential much more than if it were blasted across your profile as part of your fundamental identity.

Personalize the URL

Like most other social media sites, LinkedIn makes it possible to create a custom URL to your profile. When you first create your account, LinkedIn assigns you a random string of characters. Change it to something more personalized when you are updating your contact information at the top right section of your profile. Neglecting to replace this random string of characters with your own moniker can give the impression that you didn't know what you were doing when you created your profile.

Sidebar: What Is Work?

People often wonder whether volunteering counts as work and whether they should include volunteer positions on their profile and résumé. Without a doubt, volunteering *is* work, and you should include all appropriate volunteer activities on your profile.

The question arises because people often define "work" based solely on whether money changes hands. Why is the exchange of money the only criterion for the definition of work? What does money have to do with defining our life's work?

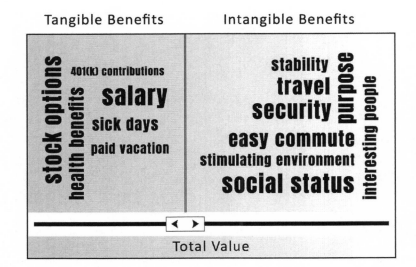

Remuneration does not define work. Work is offering something of value and being honored for that offering with something of value in return. Work is not what we get money for. Work is any activity whereby we share our talents with the world.

Think about it this way: in its most basic form, work is about offering something non-physical* that someone else values (e.g., time, talents, skills, labor) in exchange for something that you value (often including but not limited to money). Even when you are compensated financially for the value you provide, the money is never the entirety of the value that you receive in the transaction. Whenever you share your talents with the world, you also receive a host of intangible benefits. Here is a short list of some of the intangible benefits that I have received in my years of working:

- The comfort and stability of a regular paycheck (distinct from the actual money that came into my bank account);
- The security of having health benefits (distinct from the monetary value of the health insurance);
- The ability to live in an area that appealed to me;
- Social status;

---

* If we were exchanging a physical object, the transaction would be a sale.

- An environment to learn and grow both personally and professionally;
- The pleasure of associating with interesting and invigorating people;
- The opportunity to travel and experience different places;
- A sense of purpose and a platform to make an impact on the world.

How do you place a value on such things? Different people place wildly different valuations on these and many other intangible elements. Salary isn't everything. Salary isn't even close to everything when it comes to why people engage in their work every day. The weight you place on these intangibles, while highly personal, represents real value.

Which brings us back to volunteer work. In volunteer situations, while no money changes hands, there is still a significant mutual exchange of value. And this significant exchange is how we should think about work. What each party considers "of value" in the transaction is not relevant. You offer something that the other party values, and in return you receive something that you value. Money is certainly a convenient form of value, but it is far from the only one and is not required for a significant exchange of value to take place.

Consider this personal example. When I first moved to North Carolina in 2008, I was unknown in the area and unfamiliar with the economic landscape. I started volunteering for an organization of technology executives. The organization was in its early stages, and I spotted two areas in which I might be able to provide some value. First, they needed a website. Second, and more important, they needed to do some deep work on discovering who they wanted to be as an organization. Both realms are areas of expertise for me, so I signed on to volunteer for ten to fifteen hours per week. In return for my effort and expertise, I got to rub shoulders with a wide range of local technology leaders. I also claimed the title "Director of Operations," which I listed in my LinkedIn profile. The title and the opportunity to meet leaders in my field were worth far more than money to me at the time.

A second reason to include volunteer efforts in your body of work experience is that the time and effort you invest in volunteer work molds and shapes you. Volunteering is a great way to learn. Too many people think that a career is about what you have done. It isn't. A career is about what you have learned.* This is also why stumbles and failures are so valuable. We learn much more when we must wend our way through challenges and tough situations.

When a hiring manager asks about your work experience, they are trying to identify more than just what you have done. They are trying to discern what you've learned. They will be listening to your answers, reading between the lines, and trying to figure out what you've learned. I advocate downplaying the mundane details of the experience and putting the learning front and center. What you have completed is not nearly as important as what you have *learned!* Thankfully, learning has very little to do with how much you are paid, and volunteer work provides tremendous opportunities to learn.

So, yes, not only does volunteering count as work and belong on your profile, but you are also missing valuable career-development opportunities if you are not actively pursuing volunteer activities.

---

* I attribute this misdirection to lazy hiring managers who think they're looking for someone who has done the job before. Unfortunately, someone who has done the exact job before will be bored by the third week. What they need is someone who has demonstrated a capacity to learn and is ready and capable to do – or grow into — the job at hand. Discerning that readiness takes effort, insight, and a bit of risk.

Chapter 17

The Three-Pass
Method for Updating
Your Profile

Now we're going to dig into a practical technique for creating or updating the "Work History" and "Summary" sections of your LinkedIn profile. This approach will add depth and substance to an otherwise flat recounting of job descriptions. Use the same technique and most of the same information when updating your résumé, as your résumé is just a subset of your LinkedIn profile. In fact, as far as I can tell, résumés are still around only because companies insist on a Word document for their cursed applicant-tracking systems. For everyone else, your LinkedIn profile *is* your résumé.

The key is to make these updates in three distinct passes or sessions. Each pass involves a different mindset, a different way of thinking about your career and what you have done. When updating your profile, do your best to keep the different sessions separate, ideally spread across multiple days.

To Begin: Turn Off "Activity Broadcasts"

LinkedIn is an eager beaver when it comes to broadcasting your activity, and in general this is a good thing (see "Listen to Your Network" in the next chapter). If you have a good network, the people in it will be paying attention to the updates and changes you make to your profile. However, whenever you make multiple updates at once, it is wise to avoid inundating your LinkedIn network with many interim announcements about the changes. We'll turn "Activity Broadcasts" back on at the end of the process and make one more update that will be strategically telegraphed to your connections.

As of the writing of this book, the option related to **sharing profile edits** is under "Settings and Privacy." This setting allows you to choose whether your network is notified about profile changes. Toggle this to "No" for now. We'll turn this back on when we're finished.

First Pass: What Have You Done?

The first pass through your profile is to simply review and update what you have done. This is the basic résumé stuff: company, title, start date, end date, description, etc. If you think of your profile as a high-rise building, this is the core of steel and concrete upon which you will layer your career.

- Include company name, job title, start month, and end month for each position.
- Describe the basic elements of your job description.
- Highlight your responsibilities.
- Call out your results, the impact you had, the changes you were able to drive.

When listing your results, highlight both quantitative and qualitative outcomes. For example, quantitative results may be the number of people on your team. a percentage increase of sales, or total revenue. A qualitative result may be hard to put numbers on but no less significant. Perhaps you turned around a struggling team, developed a leadership team, or lead a strategic initiative.

This pass requires no deep thought and little self-reflection. It's just an accounting of what you did. This is also a good time to update all the other elements of the online profile that LinkedIn makes available, such as education, organizations, publications, patents, and so forth. These are the basic elements of a résumé or profile entry. Finish these updates and walk away for a day.

Unfortunately, this is as far as most people ever get with their profile. We're going to go much deeper—and, in the process, create a much stronger LinkedIn profile.

Second Pass: What Did You Learn?

After some time has passed and you've digested the updates you made in the first pass, sit down and take another pass at each entry in your profile. This time you are looking to add depth and color to what you have done. Make a second pass through your entries, adding what you *learned* in each role and at each company.

As I pointed out above, what you've learned is far more important than what you've done. What you have learned is everything! When an interviewer asks you questions about what you have done, they don't really care what you have done. They care about what you've learned. Make it easier for them. Spell out what you have learned right in your profile.

What You Learn Is Vastly Different From What You Do

Learning is a funny thing. It rarely happens in the moment. It almost always happens after the fact, upon reflection, and only with deliberate attention and effort.

Further, and this is the important part, the things you take away as "learnings" are often orthogonal to what you were actually doing. "Orthogonal," a word I am borrowing from mathematics, means at right angles, non-overlapping, uncorrelated, or statistically independent. What you end up learning may have very little to do with what is written in your job description.

For example, while you may be working on a tough engineering project, what you really learn is how to meet tight deadlines, manage a distributed team, or work with a tough boss. Or perhaps you are closing a big deal with a significant client. What you learn might be how to manage multiple stakeholders, listen with forensic intensity, or negotiate with poise. These learnings are orthogonal to the actual work.

And finally, not only is learning retroactive, but there's no statute of limitations on looking back and learning something new. Learning happens when you pause and reflect—at the end of the week, the end of the year, or decades later as you look back over your career. Each job is a nearly endless fount of learning, if you will just invest the time and introspection to discover what that learning is. Put it in your profile. Put it on your résumé.

Turning Bad Jobs Into Gold

As you talk about your work experience and job history, what do you do about the bad jobs? The black marks? The failed projects? The times you were let go for obtuse reasons? This is where focusing on what you've learned is much more valuable that what you've done. You've accomplished much more than you realize.

Success is a lousy teacher. When it comes to learning, there are no better teachers than challenges and adversity. When things go well, we never really know why. We think we know the reasons, but success is nuanced and complicated and we are often blind to these subtleties. Planets align. Headwinds turn into tailwinds. We get boosts from unexpected, and often unnoticed, sources. Sometimes it's as if we are swimming with the current and then proclaiming how good a swimmer we are.

I always take success stories with a grain of salt, listening for what they aren't telling me, and wondering what other factors contributed to their story. I implore you to be highly skeptical of the authors, speakers, and social media darlings who tell you that all you have to do to be successful is what they did. Skip the autobiographies of the corporate executives who promise to reveal their secrets and insights. I have no doubt that these exemplars of success have characteristics and traits that contributed to their success. Those traits might even be worth emulating. But they are far from the complete picture of how that person managed to become successful.

I once had a client who was fired from his previous two jobs. Then, due to deeply personal reasons, he took a couple of years off from the workforce. When we sat down together and thoroughly worked through what happened at each job, we discovered that both were a goldmine of learning. Tough clients and deals that had faltered offered tremendous insights into how to do things differently next time. And the two years away from work helped him to forge a personal level of wisdom and awareness that was invaluable as he returned to the workforce. It took nine months to process and regroup, but he landed on his feet with an innovative company in Silicon Valley and went on to take a leading role in their sales organization.

Knowledge is knowing the rules. Wisdom is knowing the exceptions. It is essential that you uncover your own learnings and articulate them in your résumé and LinkedIn profile. I recommend one or two bullets in each section that begin with "Learned…" Friends, colleagues, former colleagues, coaches, and therapists can all be valuable resources to help you uncover what you have learned. You have more insight and wisdom to offer than you realize.

Third Pass: What Are You Ready For?

Many people consider only their recent work history when choosing their next job, whether it's another position internally or at a new company. This is shortsighted. Why would you want to do more of what you've already done? I'd be bored. It's demotivating to keep doing the same things over and over. Humans are creatures of growth and challenge. You want to advance your career based not on what you've done but on what you are ready to do next.

Recruiters and hiring managers often talk about looking for career progression on a résumé. This means they are looking for a pattern of applying what you have learned in one role to being successful in the next. This is rarely obvious, perhaps not even to you. Do your best to spell it out in your profile. Make it easy for the recruiters and hiring managers who are looking for a career progression as they move chronologically through your résumé. List at least one bullet under each company (or position) describing what you were preparing yourself to do. If you are lucky, what you were ready for at the end of one role will be what you were doing at the beginning of the next one. It doesn't always work out that way, and that's okay. We're looking for broad trends here.

It does not matter if what you were ready for and what you did next were not intentional at the time you were engaged in the work. Very few people have a career path that unfolds in a straight line. Like learning, discovering what you were ready for often happens retrospectively as well. It is perfectly valid to superimpose a narrative over your career that is derived with the benefits of hindsight and the wisdom of experience.

Summary Section

After you have updated all your work experience, fill in the "Summary" section at the top of your LinkedIn profile with broad strokes of who you are and what you are ready for. It should include anything that you want someone else — especially someone in a position to hire you — to know. This may be key skills, major accomplishments, significant credentials, values, aspirations, and so forth.

Hold your résumé at arm's length and ask yourself, "What are the two or three things that I want every hiring manager to take away from a ninety-second review of my résumé?" Don't rely solely on your own perspective. Ask trusted advisors to name three things they see in you that everyone should know. Whatever those two or three things turn out to be, make sure they are prominently expressed in the "Summary" section of your LinkedIn profile.

I recommend leading off your "Summary" section with your elevator pitch. The best way to compose an introductory statement is to weave the answers to the following three questions into one or two sentences.

1. Who are the kinds of people that can benefit from the value that you have to offer? To whom can you be helpful?

2. What situation do these people find themselves in when you are able to help them?

3. What kinds of results do you deliver for these people?

For example, the description of what I do in my coaching services might go something like this:

> *I work with ambitious professionals in mid to late career who feel stuck and want more from their jobs and their lives. We work together on leadership development, team building, time management, career strategy, executive presence, getting unstuck, getting promoted, navigating the subtle nuances of large organizations, and figuring out what they should do with their lives.*

Can you see how I wove the answers to the three questions into those two sentences?

Notify Your Network About Your New Profile

Now that your profile updates are complete, we're going to announce the new you. You're going to turn "Activity Broadcasts" back on and then make two key changes to your profile that will be telegraphed to your network. Go back to "Settings and Privacy" in your account, and set "Activity Broadcasts" to "Yes." Then make two more updates to your profile:

1. Update your profile photo (see Chapter 16 for guidelines).

2. Edit your headline. This is the field directly under your name on your LinkedIn profile. If you like the headline you have, just make a small change and then undo it. We want LinkedIn to think that you have changed your headline.

With "Activity Broadcasts" back on, the people in your network will be notified of these last two updates through LinkedIn's usual emails and notifications. This is a good thing.

Think about how powerful this is. What do *you* do when you receive an email from LinkedIn telling you that someone in your network has updated their profile photo or title? You must admit that the urge to click and see the new photo or title is irresistible. You are essentially having an asynchronous conversation without words between you and the people who are paying attention in your network.

Recommendations

Your LinkedIn profile is a public proclamation of who you are as a professional. However, this proclamation is in a single voice: yours. Recommendations complement that declaration in multiple voices and from different perspectives. I find them invaluable when I am trying to get a sense of a person's character and personality, and especially when I am preparing to meet someone for the first time.

At one point the LinkedIn Help Pages offered this great advice for recommendations. The text is no longer on the site, but the advice still stands:

> The best recommendations come from people who value your work, services or products, such as managers, colleagues, co-workers, customers, and clients. Hiring managers and people searching for new customers and business partners prefer to work with people who come recommended by someone they know and trust.[42]

While some recommendations come to you unsolicited, it is best to ask for recommendations from a few of your key first-degree connections. Here are a few guidelines:

1. Be judicious in who you select to provide a recommendation. You are asking for a favor. It takes time and mental effort on their behalf for the person to write the recommendation.

2. Choose people who can illuminate your strengths from a different perspective.

3. Provide prompts and suggestions on what they might include in their recommendation. I usually include a statement along the lines, "While I encourage you to write whatever comes to mind, I was thinking that you might make a few comments on..." fill in the blank.

4. You will have the opportunity to accept and display the recommendation after they write it.

5. Avoid quid pro quo recommendations: "I'll recommend you if you recommend me." I often click on a recommendation and see if there is a reciprocal recommendation from you on the other person's profile. If there is, the overall impact of the recommendation is greatly reduced.

Aim for a minimum of five recommendations sprinkled across the various positions in your profile. And of course, don't forget that writing a recommendation for someone in your network is a tremendous way to strengthen the connection between you.

Exercise: Update Your LinkedIn Profile

Do it! You know what to do now. Follow the guidelines and recommendations in this chapter. What are you waiting for?*

---

* As with all of the exercises in this book, this exercise — spelled out in step-by-step detail — is included in *The Workbook of Helpful Exercises*, which can be downloaded at heatherhollick.com/helpful.

Chapter 18

Leveraging LinkedIn

*Most of the successful people I've known are the
ones who do more listening than talking.*

Bernard Baruch

While your LinkedIn profile stands as a testament to who you are as a professional, the entire LinkedIn site—brought to life by your network of connections—is a vibrant hub of communication with the people in your network. The key is to strike a balance between listening, engaging, and broadcasting.

Listen To Your Network

Through a well-rounded suite of email options and a home page newsfeed, LinkedIn does a decent job of alerting you to who's active in your network. The home page is an endless stream of ideas, articles, and events that are important in the lives of people you have deemed to be important to you.* Skim this regularly, commenting on posts when you are so inclined. And reach out privately to anyone who reminds you that the freshness meter on your relationship has dropped below the level of acceptability.

In addition to the newsfeed on the home page, which you must remember to visit, LinkedIn does an admirable job of pushing information via email that is highly relevant to your networking activity.

---

* I fully acknowledge that LinkedIn's home page is also an endless stream of promoted posts. I will be among the first to sign up for an ad-free version of their service, should they ever offer one. Until then, I do my best to look past the sponsored material.

I opt to receive almost all the communication options so that I get a steady stream of concise emails alerting me to activity in my network: promotions, job changes, birthdays, work anniversaries, or the simple fact that someone has viewed my profile. Any of these announcements are perfect opportunities to freshen the connection. These are the people who are letting you know that they are active in their careers and in their network. A brief note of congratulations or a well-timed inquiry of "What are you working on?" goes a long way toward keeping your network alive and fresh.

Regular Active Review

The links in your network can grow quickly grow stale. It takes energy and commitment to keep the right connections fresh. In that vein, I thoroughly review my entire list of LinkedIn connections on a regular basis. A couple of times per year — over the course of a few days — I pour over my connections. I sort "My Network" alphabetically by last name and ask myself a series of questions about each person:

1. What are they working on?
2. Do I need to freshen or strengthen the network link with this person?
3. Do I know something that might help this person be successful?
4. Do I know someone who should meet this person, or vice versa?
5. Should I write them a recommendation?
6. Has this connection gone dormant? That is, has the time come to disconnect from this person?*

---

* LinkedIn does not notify a person when you disconnect from them. Your network comprises people you know well enough to recommend with confidence. If you are connected to people on LinkedIn for whom that is no longer true, don't think of it as "unfriending" them. Think of it as actively culling your network to keep it manageable. This activity is as important as adding new connections.

Talk To Your Network

In the early days of the internet, before the world wide web and long before the advent of social media, to be online meant being a part of one or more online discussion forums. Usenet newsgroups were among the first.[43] Corporate enterprises like Prodigy, CompuServe, and eventually, AOL joined the fray and sought to commercialize the venture.

In addition to participating in a few Usenet newsgroups, I opted for CompuServe as my first home on the internet, primarily for the breadth and depth of their computer-centric forums and discussion groups. In those early days I was an active member of the forum for the HP 95LX, a portable PC that fit in the palm of your hand and ran MS-DOS and a full version of Lotus 1-2-3.* These were early days for computers of any kind, let alone ones that ran on AA batteries and slid into a pocket or purse. Members from all over the world shared their insights and joy with one another.

While I don't remember the substance of a single discussion, I vividly recall the joy and magic I felt as part of an online community. People, on their own schedules and scattered around the world, engaged in asynchronous, slow-motion conversation. While most of our dialogue centered around tech-talk, we frequently ventured off topic, supporting one another in the joys and challenges of life.† This was my tribe.

Social media has capitalized on this magic, making it possible for us to engage in numerous slow-motion conversations on platforms ranging from messaging apps to Facebook. Not to be left out, LinkedIn is not shy about giving you opportunities to communicate with your network. Across the top of your home page is a prominent box prompting you to share an article, photo, video, or idea. Activity on any of these fronts will give you an opportunity to talk to your network. Post a

---

* The 95LX and its descendants, the 200LX and the 600LX, were amazing devices at the pre-dawn of portable computing. See "HP 95LX," *Wikipedia*, bit.ly/helpful_95LX.

† For example, I was a cigarette smoker in those days and finally made the decision to quit once and for all. The daily support of my forum friends was invaluable, especially during the first week as I withdrew from the addictive shackles of nicotine.

status update, click "Like," or make a comment in a group discussion, and your network will be notified. This is a good thing.

Status Updates

Like Facebook, LinkedIn's options to share an article, photo, video, or idea allow you to share with your network where you are and what you are doing. Unlike Facebook, however, the decorum on LinkedIn is decidedly professional. Updates revolve around what you're working on, what you're pondering, and what you're recommending. In general, it is wise to save the baby pictures and vacation photos for other social media sites. I think of it as slow-motion small talk. Like small talk in face-to-face encounters, each status update or interaction with connections in your timeline is a volley in a potential conversation that could go deeper—just like the two old modems negotiating the possibility of a conversation.

I recommend posting regularly, especially when you want to signal to your network that you are engaged. If you write for a blog or post relevant professional content elsewhere on the web, let your network know via a status update. Assume they are as engaged as you are. Help them help you by keeping your network apprised of what you are working on and what you are thinking. And be prepared to engage with people who engage with you. It is, after all, an asynchronous, slow-motion conversation.

Passive Signaling

People get notified when you view their profile (this is a setting in "Communication Preferences"; the default is "On"). This is a good thing. I keep this option turned on and use it strategically:

- Someone will pop into my mind for whatever reason, and I will click on their LinkedIn profile to refresh my memory, check on where they are now, and see if I can discern what they are working on. The notification they receive from LinkedIn that I have viewed their profile is a nice way of letting them know that I have been thinking of them.

- I look up the names of people at upcoming conferences or meetings I will be attending. Not only am I more likely to make a deeper connection when I eventually meet some of these people face-to-face, but they will get the notification—with a glimpse of my picture—before we meet in person.

- Similarly, if you are preparing for an interview, look up all the names of the people you will be talking to a day or two before the scheduled interview. Not only will you be better prepared for the interview, but also, within a week each person will get a ping from LinkedIn that you have viewed their profile. This will help you stay top of mind days after the interview is over.

Finally, when people view my profile I usually reciprocate, asking myself, "Is this a person I should reach out to? Why would they have been looking at my profile? How can I help them be successful?"

Avoid LIONs

Since the earliest days of LinkedIn (2003) there has been ongoing debate over the quality versus quantity of connections. On the quantity side are the LIONs, the LinkedIn Open Networkers. LIONs generally accept all invitations to connect and do not mark invitations as spam or "I don't know" (both of which can result in LinkedIn potentially penalizing the inviter, with actions ranging from requiring the person to know the email addresses of future invitees to marking the account as spam and closing it).[44]

I am not a LION. Open networkers are operating from a fundamentally different premise of a network. Back in Chapter 6 we defined a network as the living organism formed by the links between you and all the people you know, given life by the freshness and strength of those links. If you don't know someone, if you don't even have the vaguest sense of what they are working on, then by our definition, they are not part of your network.

In contrast to open networkers, I see my LinkedIn network as an online reflection of the active connections I maintain with people in real life. I limit my connections to the people I know well enough to recommend with confidence. As a result, I am discerning when it comes to accepting unsolicited invitations to connect. I prefer to accept invitations to connect with people I have met in person or, at least, by telephone. If we have not yet met, I may invite you to engage via a phone or Skype call if it looks like we might be able to develop a mutually beneficial relationship. Most of the time, however, I simply ignore unsolicited invitations.

Until recently, LinkedIn was specific about not condoning open networkers. At one time they included the following sage advice as part of their extensive list of Do's and Don'ts in their User Agreement:[45]

- Don't invite people you do not know to join your network.

- Don't use LinkedIn invitations to send messages to people who don't know you or who are unlikely to recognize you as a known contact.

Even though this language has been scrubbed from their pages, the wisdom that it embodies remains. With a network of quality, known connections I can avail myself of LinkedIn's features to listen to my network. I use LinkedIn not as a business platform but as a community that I have constructed so that I can pay attention to the updates and goings-on of the people in that community. This helps me know how I might be helpful and anticipate how they might be helpful to me. I lose the affinity to my tribe — and the desire to pay attention — if I connect with people I do not know.

There are other platforms across the internet where I can broadcast to untold thousands, even millions. LinkedIn is an online database of my real-life connections. It is the place where I engage with my network; for that reason, I limit my connections to those with whom I want to engage.

Personalize Your Connection Request

Strive to always send a personalized invitation when requesting to connect with someone. I cringe whenever I get an invitation with the default message stating, "I'd like to connect with you on LinkedIn" and nothing else. There is no indication of where we met, how we know each other, or why they think it might be good for us to connect. This seems to be a highly impersonal way to start a personal relationship.

LinkedIn is mostly to blame for these impersonal connection requests. Personalizing the invitation is easier said than done. If you send an invitation from any of their mobile apps or from most of the "Connect" links on their website, the invitation will be generic.

The surest way to have the option to personalize your invitation is to use a web browser and drill into the potential connection's full profile. LinkedIn prominently displays a "Connect" button next to the profile of anyone not already in your network. If you are viewing the person's full LinkedIn profile, this button will pop up a screen allowing you to personalize your connection request.

However, as of this writing, *any other time you click the "Connect" button* while in the LinkedIn universe, you will *not* have an opportunity to customize the message. That means if you are using one of the LinkedIn mobile apps and you are lured by the convenience of tapping "Connect," don't do it. The initiation will be whisked away before you have a chance to personalize your message. Or perhaps you are scrolling through LinkedIn's list of "People You May Know" on the website and you see a button underneath each person's headshot that says "Connect." Don't click it; you won't get a chance to customize your invitation. Similarly, if you're looking at a screen of search results and you see the blue "Connect" box on the right side, well, you know what happens. Don't click it. The inherently personal nature of a LinkedIn connection makes it worthwhile to always try to send a warm, personalized invitation.

You would think that a site dedicated to maintaining relationships would make it easier to get those relationships off to a good start. Go figure. I sometimes wonder whether they understand that the tool they have created serves as a lubricant for a near-infinite number of interpersonal relationships. At times it seems as if LinkedIn's right hand isn't sure what its left hand is doing. Until they figure it out, always start from the full view of a person's profile before initiating a connection request.*

Should I Pay For a Premium Account?

In a word, yes. If you find LinkedIn valuable, then honor that value by paying for a premium account. This is how the world is supposed to work. That's certainly how I want it to work for me, and I hope it's how you want it to work for you. If you find value in something, honor that value in a way that seems appropriate to you. For an online service, paying for a premium level of service honors the value that you receive from them.

Of course, there are more reasons to pay for a LinkedIn account than simply to feel good about yourself and your role in the global economy. Like most online services, LinkedIn offers several tiers with more features available in various paid plans.[46] Of the ten or more features available on the plans, only two are of interest to me and I find them indispensable:

- **Who's Viewed Your Profile**: The free plan has limited visibility into who has viewed your profile. I check who has viewed my profile at least once a week. These are people who have expressed an interest in me for one reason or another. I frequently reach out to these people, freshening old connections or proposing new ones. Since knowing who has viewed my profile is one of the key ways I "listen" to my network, this feature alone is worth the admission price of a premium plan.

- **Full Profiles**: The free tier limits you to seeing the full profiles only up to your second-degree connections. This will give you visibility into tens and perhaps hundreds of thousands of connections. However, paid plans offer you full profiles of everyone in your network: first-, second-, third-degree, and

---

* Over the years I have passed on this feedback to LinkedIn via multiple channels. I'm not sure whether their business model or their software-development priorities have kept this request from being implemented. Nevertheless, I will persist.

group connections. This will expand the number of visible profiles into the tens and perhaps hundreds of *millions!*

Share Your Connections

You can control who sees your connections in your privacy settings. You have the option to make them visible to "Only You" or all of your first-degree connections via "Your Connections." I recommend setting this to "Your Connections." I am delighted when one person in my network discovers that they want to meet someone else in my network. My goal is to share who and what I know with others. To my knowledge, none of my connections have ever abused this feature, and if that were ever to happen, I would simply disconnect from the abuser.*

How Large Is Your Network?

With each new connection you make on LinkedIn, the size of your accessible network grows exponentially. Once you have more than a few hundred connections, the number of people within your reach will astound you. In my own case, after almost fourteen years on LinkedIn, I have direct or indirect access to almost 1.25 *million* people! Granted, I have been on LinkedIn for a long time and now have almost 1,000 people in my network, but I noticed a significant improvement in the quality of my search results when I crossed the threshold of 250 connections.

For all practical purposes, you have an accessible network comprising your first- and second-degree connections. LinkedIn is always eager to show you your third-degree connections as well, but since you don't know those people and are not connected to anyone who does, they are of marginal value in a networking sense. For this reason, I only consider first- and second-degree connections as part of my "accessible" network. With a well-nurtured web of first-degree connections,

---

* This is another reason why I am judicious in deciding whether to connect with someone. By only connecting with people I know well enough to recommend with confidence, I have never worried that any of those connections would be exploited.

the combination of your first- and second-degree connections will be a rich asset to your career.

Imagine this scenario: you are looking for a contact at company X. You are thinking of applying for a job there and want to ask someone a few questions about the culture. You go to LinkedIn, put the name of the company in the search bar, and skim the results. LinkedIn will return a list of first-, second-, and third-degree connections. Filter the results to only first- and second-degree connections, and be prepared to be amazed.

For example, I have only two first-degree connections who currently work at Hewlett Packard. However, I have more than 1,600 second-degree connections! Each of these 1,600 second-degree connections is connected to someone I know.

Not only are these 1,600 people connected to someone I know, but because I have been careful to connect only with people I know well enough to recommend with confidence, I would also have no qualms about asking my connections for an introduction to one of these second-degree connections.

This is the driving factor of my LinkedIn strategy, and I can't emphasize it enough. Connecting with anyone willy-nilly does not give you a meaningful connection with even the first-degree connections, let alone the people to whom they might give you access. But if you carefully curate your connections, if you connect only with people you know with some degree of confidence, and if you maintain a minimal level of freshness with all these connections, then you will have a phenomenal number of people accessible to you in your network.

Counting Connections

How many meaningful connections do you have? In the early days, LinkedIn provided a dashboard showing your network statistics, which included your current number of first-, second-, and third-degree connections. Unfortunately, that functionality was removed a few years ago. However, it's easy to get an estimate of your total number of connections by using the search function.

The count of your first-degree connections is easy: it's prominently displayed when you view "My Network" from the main menu bar. To get a reasonable estimate of the number of your second- and third-degree connections, simply search for a very common word, such as "the," which is likely to be on just about everyone's profile. Now use the filter options that appear on the right side of the search results to limit the results to only your second-degree connections. The total count, representing a good approximation, will be at the top of the search results.

Leveraging the LinkedIn Bridge

Most people think that the number of connections they have on LinkedIn includes only their first-degree connections. Au contraire. Don't sell yourself short. If you have built your network with integrity, then your number of potentially helpful connections includes both your first- and second-degree connections, giving you access to hundreds of thousands, if not millions, of people.

To illustrate how this works and what I mean by your "accessible network," let's return to our scenario of looking for a contact at company X. If you have been limiting your LinkedIn connections to people you know well enough to recommend with confidence, then all your first-degree connections at this company are people you know well enough to ask for a favor: fifteen minutes of their time for a quick call to talk about their company culture.

You will, however, have exponentially more second-degree connections than first-degree ones, and **all the second-degree connections are linked to people you know!** In this case you are going to ask your second-degree connections for a slightly different favor. Since you can't be sure that all your first-degree connections share the same LinkedIn philosophy that you do—to only connect with people you know well enough to recommend with confidence—you want to send a slightly more nuanced request for a favor. The email that I compose usually sounds something like this:

Dear Suzie,

I see that you are connected on LinkedIn to Bob Smith at company X. How well do you know him? Do you by chance know him well enough to introduce me?

I am looking to talk to someone about the culture at Company X, and Bob looks interesting. If you feel comfortable introducing me, I'll send along a separate note that you could forward as part of the introduction. If not, no worries; I'll keep exploring.

Many thanks,

Heather

This is what I call the LinkedIn Bridge. The incredible reach of your first-degree connections is precisely the reason you want to be so protective of those connections, limiting them to people you know with some degree of confidence. By doing so, you will be able to reach *through* these first-degree connections to hundreds of thousands of people across every imaginable industry and geography.

On a final note, I always send these kinds of messages via email, rather than using LinkedIn's internal messaging system. These are first-degree connections, after all. If I don't have their email address in my personal address book, I can always check their profile to see what email addresses they have on LinkedIn. Emails are easier to forward, creating a thread of credibility.

Ideally, the person you are contacting will forward one of your emails, with her introduction, to the person you are trying to reach. This is an efficient way to get a warm, credible introduction to someone. Plus, people get a cacophony of messages from countless apps and websites these days. When it comes to business, careers, and professional networking, email is still the default messaging platform.

Exercise: LinkedIn Network Review

I recommend reviewing your LinkedIn connections from A to Z at least twice per year. If you have many connections, you might want to spread the exercise over a few days or weeks.*

- From the home screen on LinkedIn, click on "My Network" and then on "See All" under the count of your network connections in the upper left part of the screen.
- Sort by "Last Name."

Spend a few minutes looking at each of your contacts. Click on their profile and ask yourself the following questions for each person:

- How do I know this person? Where or when did we meet?
- Is this person still a part of my active network? If not, should I cull this connection?
- What are they working on?
- Does this link need to be freshened?
- Is now a good time to update them on what I'm working on?
- Do I wish that this link were stronger? If so, what can I do to strengthen it?
- Is there something that I know, perhaps an article that I have read, that I could share with this person?
- Is there someone in my network to whom I could introduce them? Or vice versa?

Bonus Exercise: How large is your network?

Search for the word "the" in the global search box on LinkedIn. On the "Results" page, filter by your first- and second-degree connections. Note the total number of connections. For all practical purposes, this is the size of your active network.

---

* All of the exercises in this book are included in *The Workbook of Helpful Exercises*, which can be downloaded at heatherhollick.com/helpful.

Chapter 19

Mastering Meetings and Events

All the world's a stage,
And all the men and women merely players;
They have their exits and their entrances,
And one man in his time plays many parts,

William Shakespeare, *As You Like It, Act II, Scene V*

In this chapter we will talk about large meetings and events. We have already covered significant ground on how to prepare for a one-on-one meeting. Everything we have said so far still holds:

- Research people in advance so that you can make deeper connections more quickly. Start with their LinkedIn profile.

- Help people help you. Get a sense of who will be there, so you can answer the question "What are *you* working on?" in a way that might interest the people you will meet.

- Follow up.

Now we explore — especially from the perspective of people with a preference for introversion — attending meetings, events, and conferences. While everything we cover applies equally to extraverts, introverts often face unique challenges at large conferences, workshops, and networking events.

Before: Preparation

Do Your Homework

Preparing to meet people one-on-one is easy. You know who you'll be meeting with, so you look them up, refresh your memory, anticipate their questions, and prepare your elevator pitch. However, when you attend large events, there's no specific person to look up in advance. Or is there? Some creativity is in order.

Finding the names of people you want to research may require a bit of sleuthing. Here are a few guidelines:

- Given the nature of the event, what *kinds* of people will be attending? In general, what are their interests and preferences?

- Do you know the organizers? Look them up.

- Will there be speakers? Research them. If you don't have the time to read their books, at least read a couple of the reviews.

- Is there a list of attendees for the event? Registration systems like Eventbrite and MeetUp have the option to make the list of attendees available to all the participants. Learn a bit about the background of anyone who looks interesting.

- Have there been any mass emails to the attendees? Sometimes you can get the names of other attendees from information in the email.

- Finally, what kinds of people are you *hoping* to meet at the event? Prepare to meet one of those people.

Prepare Your Game Plan

Once you have done your homework on who might be attending an event, the next step is to think about why you are going and what you might get out of the experience. Have a game plan for every meeting and event[*] that you attend. Show up with intent. What do you hope

---

[*] This "game plan" template works equally well for all meetings, regardless of their members or purpose.

will happen at this meeting or event? Who do you think you might meet here? What will you say to them?

A good game plan includes three important elements: your objective for the meeting, the key outcomes you expect, and the anticipated next steps. Of course, *actual outcomes* and next steps may vary dramatically, but it is valuable to have a starting point as you go into the meeting.

- **Objective**: Why am I meeting with this person or attending this event? Be realistic—and modest. You are likely there to learn something. But you are also there to meet people, to find people with whom you can share your knowledge and your network, and to look for people who are looking for you.

- **Key outcomes**: What can I reasonably expect to happen?

- **Next steps**: What will be (or what are) the next steps?

With a solid game plan, you can engage in more meaningful conversations more quickly because you will have a clear sense of purpose for your presence there. Once a good conversation is underway, the key outcomes—hovering in the back of your mind—will guide you with a sense of how you might want to steer the conversations. Finally, having given some thought to what next steps you hope for, you can move in for the "close" of a conversation that ensures the interaction will be mutually beneficial.

Best of all, having achieved your objectives—or definitively concluded that they will not be met—you will know when it's time to leave. You can exit gracefully and confidently, knowing that you have either accomplished what you set out to accomplish or that there is no use wasting any more time trying.

Prepare Your Introduction

Anticipate that, while striking up conversations, people will offer you the opportunity to share what you are working on. It usually happens at that magic moment when you have made it through the small talk and you are pivoting to a potentially more meaningful conversation. This is a golden opportunity. Don't miss it, and for goodness' sake, don't take it lightly. Be prepared. I work on my introduction as I am traveling to the event. I may have given it some thought much further in advance, but I always spend some time en route framing and polishing what I will say when asked about myself.

As you recall from our initial discussion, not everyone is a savvy networker, and some people may phrase the transitional question as, "What do you do?" or "What brings you here?" When someone asks, "What do you do?", don't just tell them what you do. The question is closed-ended, rarely leading to engaging dialogue. Instead, pretend that they asked you a more open-ended question. Come prepared to respond with a couple of sentences that will give people a sense of who you are and the impact you aspire to have on the world. For example, don't recite your job title; tell them the kinds of people you work with and the ways in which you help them.

Regardless of how the question is worded, your best, most mutually productive answer is something you are working on — at home, at work, or in your career. Assume that their intentions, like yours, are to be helpful, and give them something to work with. Good networkers will be intrigued and will try to respond in a helpful way.

Your conversations will vary depending on the context. As you prepare, think about the kinds of people you will likely meet and the information, connections, or resources they might have. Frame your thoughts based on what they may find interesting. People want to be helpful, but you must meet them halfway.

Some people might call this your "elevator pitch," but I've never liked the term. It's not a *pitch*. You're not trying to sell something. In a networking situation you are simply trying to engage another human being in a meaningful conversation that might lead to the exchange of favors or information and, ideally, an ongoing, mutually beneficial relationship.

Get in the Right Mindset

Although we don't often think of it as such, socializing is a performance. We choose a role, adopt a persona, and enter the arena of social interactions. Most people, especially extraverts, do this automatically, without giving it a second thought.

Introverts, on the other hand, can be at a distinct disadvantage when it comes to socializing. They do their best work inside their heads, where thoughts and ideas reign supreme and where personas and attitudes are never judged or, more important, misinterpreted. When it comes to interacting with the outside world, the introvert's rich inner world does not always translate into warm, convivial interactions.

Regardless of where you fall on the spectrum of introversion and extraversion, it is in your best interest to deliberately and consciously choose the persona that you want to embody for the event. Invest a few moments to "get in character," as an actor might say as she prepares to step onto the stage.

First, decide how you want to be perceived, how you want to carry yourself, and in general, how you want to *be.* How do you want people to feel when they first meet you? What do you want them to think about you? How do you want to be remembered? Visualize yourself as that person.

Second, get yourself in a positive, upbeat frame of mind. Positive energy is much more powerful and effective for connecting with people. This is especially true in North America, where the culture has a bias for extraversion and the default, if not expected, behavior is upbeat and gregarious.

As an introvert, my interior and exterior worlds are not always perfectly aligned. I can be savoring several deep trains of thought while the look on my face is often somber, if not sullen. To remedy this mismatch, I turn to music or comedy.

I have two playlists on my iPhone that are specifically crafted for when I need to give my exterior persona a boost. One playlist is full of songs that get my blood flowing and pump me up. Over the years, these songs have proven so effective at getting me in a good mood that merely starting to sing a few notes of one of the songs is enough to lift my spirits or get me through the TSA line without attracting undue scrutiny.

The other playlist is a selection of some of my favorite comedy clips. Although I have heard these routines dozens of times, they still make me smile. They are the perfect pick-me-up as I prepare to engage with other people. I almost always play selections from one or both while I am en route to a networking event.

During: Performance

As mentioned above, showing up at meetings, events, and conferences is akin to an actor walking onstage. You've practiced your lines and gotten "in character." Now the curtain is up, the stage is lit, and it is time to perform. Here are some tips and tricks that will improve your performance.

Travel Light

Keep at least one hand free. Avoid the temptation to weigh yourself down with all manner of food and beverage, napkins, notebooks, handouts, and handbags. Shaking hands is an important ritual, particularly in America and other western cultures.* I recommend leaning in to a good handshake when meeting someone (while you say, "It is very nice to meet you") and again as you part (when you say, "It has been a pleasure talking to you"). If you're holding a drink or a plate of food, make sure you can inconspicuously set it down or shuffle it to your left hand to free up the right side of your body to engage in the all-important handshakes.

Invest the time to learn how to master a good handshake. There is no better teacher here than Mark Horstman of "Manager Tools."† His Hall of Fame Guidance titled "The Secrets of a Great Handshake" is

---

* In many cultures greetings other than handshakes are more appropriate, such as bowing, hugging, or kisses on the cheek. The physicality of these varied greetings serves to underscore the need to keep one or both hands free in social situations.

† Having started a weekly podcast in the early days of podcasting, Mark Horstman and Michael Auzenne have built "Manager Tools" into an incredible array of career resources. I can't recommend it highly enough. See **manager-tools.com** for all they have to offer.

worth every minute of your time.[47] Mark explains, among many vivid and surprising details about a great handshake, how you want to lean in with your left shoulder, rotating slightly as you extend your right hind, find the webbing between your thumb and forefinger, and connect that confidently with the webbing between their thumb and forefinger as you firmly grab their hand, pump once or twice up and down, and let go. This is the realm of business. And there are no gender variations in handshakes. Mark is adamant that both men and women should engage in equally firm—not painful or "crusher"—grips.

Regardless of your native culture, the handshake is the most important professional greeting in modern business. Doing one well not only makes a great first impression, but it also incorporates the powerful element of touch into the relationship.

Use Business Cards

Regardless of where you are in your career, I believe business cards are a must. I never leave home without them. Names can be hard. Handing someone a business card means they are less likely to forget you and more likely to follow up.

The advent of smartphones has tempted many people to skip the card and go straight to electronic records. Resist this temptation. Bumping phones or stopping to enter your contact information in the other person's address book is a huge distraction and disrupts the flow of conversation.

Keep it simple. An elegant, unobtrusive exchange of business cards is an art. Most important, the exchange of token physical objects makes it almost sacred. When someone offers me a card, I am grateful. I look at it, register their name in my brain, and gently put it in my pocket.

Your business cards don't have to be fancy, although paying a professional graphic designer to create one for you will be worth the investment. At the very least, your card should include an email address and phone number. Including your Twitter handle and your custom link to your LinkedIn profile (e.g., LinkedIn.com/in/hhollick) is not uncommon.

Finally, when attending an event where you know you will meet new people, make sure your cards are easily accessible. Fumbling around to find a card breaks the spell. Have them readily accessible in a pocket or purse, ideally so you can grab one without even looking. Of course, you should also expect to receive business cards in return. Have a separate pocket designated where you will quickly stash any business cards you receive.

Wear a Name Tag

A name tag makes you more approachable and serves as a visual hook that will reinforce the name that people hear when you introduce yourself. If the name tags are handwritten, write your first name only in large, easy-to-read letters. Skip your last name — it's on your business card — or write it in much smaller letters. The goal is to be remembered, not legally complete, and your first name alone is much easier to remember than both your first and last names.

Clothing and lanyards permitting,* place the name tag over your right chest. If you are right-handed, this may seem counterintuitive. Your natural inclination is to take the name tag in your dominant hand and slap it on your left chest. This is suboptimal.

To understand why, think about the body mechanics as two people shake hands. In this brief cultural dance, two people turn slightly toward each other, lean in slightly, reach out their right hands, and clasp them. If the name tag is on the right chest, it is directly in your line of sight as you extend your right arm. It is the most natural thing in the world, as the two right hands are coming together, to raise your eyes slightly and glance at the other person's name tag, thus linking in your mind the physical sensation of shaking their hand with the visual representation of their name.

However, what happens in that moment of the handshake if the name tag is on the other person's *left* shoulder? Your bodies are slightly turned and your right arms are extended. To look at the name tag, you

---

* If you find yourself at an event where you have no choice but to wear your name tag on a lanyard hung around your neck, check periodically to make sure that your name is facing outward. Just sayin'.

must turn your head slightly to the right and look across their body for their name tag. This is awkward, to say the least. Regardless of whether you are left or right-handed, wear your name tag on your right chest.

Work the Room

When I was younger, the thought of entering a room full of people and striking up a conversation terrified me. I could usually muster enough courage to enter the room, but once inside, I was almost catatonic, standing along the wall—often just inside the door—trying to figure out what I should say or do next. The amount of stress I felt would escalate in sync with the volume of the voices in the room—the louder the volume, the more paralyzed I became.

To get over my stress, I tried an experiment. Over the course of several months, I tried to adopt a different objective when attending networking events. Rather than worry about who I would talk to and what I would say, I took a time-out. Instead of talking, I decided to simply stand there, watch, and listen.

I entered rooms in my usual discomfited way, but instead of fretting about jumping into conversations, I just stood there. Quietly. Not worrying. I used one of the gifts of my introversion to "read the room." What was happening here? What was *trying* to happen? Where was the energy? Where were the centers of gravity? How were different people working the room differently?

The results of my observations were amazing. Not only did different people work the room very differently, but the variety of styles and preferences made the event interesting and vibrant. As a result of my ongoing experiment, the rest of this chapter reflects my new rules for working a room.

Honor Your Preferences

Savvy introverts and extraverts will work a room very differently. It is natural for the extraverts to gravitate to the center of the room, picking up conversations along the way. This is how extraverts *should* work a room. It's how they get their bearings and find their energy. They bring the initial spark to the room.

It is no less natural, however, for an introvert to pause just inside the door and observe. The key is to be not paralyzed but confident; not fearful but curious. This is how introverts get *their* bearings and find *their* energy. By honoring our strengths and preferences, we are both doing what we do best. It won't take long before you find yourself engrossed in interesting conversations that you have either initiated or joined. If you have a preference for introversion, more often than not people will come to you. You don't have to push yourself to the center of the room if you don't want to. People will find you where you are.

If the room is too noisy to hear yourself think, step out to a quieter place. How in the world can you expect to make any kind of human connection in an atmosphere where you can't even hear your own thoughts, let alone the voices of the other people? On more than one occasion I have stepped out of a busy conference hall and into a quieter lobby, only to have a small cadre of like-minded networkers follow suit. The calmer environment made for much more productive networking.

Small Talk Is... Small Talk

I used to beat myself up when the opening volleys of my conversation were awkward. As in the movies, if only I had been more erudite or witty, the conversations would have taken off with grace. But real life never plays out like an Aaron Sorkin script. What I observed is that all small talk is awkward and stilted. Everyone has these monosyllabic entrances into the freeways of conversation:

"Hey."

"What's up?"

"Not much, what brings you here?"

"How about this weather?"

You get the idea. As I noted earlier, don't sweat small talk. It's always awkward and it doesn't always work. When small talk works, great, segue into a more productive conversation. If it doesn't work, smile and move on. In either case, don't worry about it.

Watch the Body Language

Not only do individuals tell a story with their body language—arms crossed, shoulders slouched, for example—but *groups* of people tell stories as well. When you are looking for a conversation to join, read the signals of the group before inserting yourself.

For example, when two people are standing face-to-face, squared off directly across from each other, they are engaged in a closed conversation. The positions of their bodies subconsciously signal that interruptions are not welcome in that moment. Look for pairs of people standing in a more inviting "V" formation. This open arrangement of their feet signals that new members are welcome in the conversation.

Similarly, a group of three or more people standing in a closed circle is not open to new members. Look for groups in a "U" shape with an opening at one end. That opening is for you. Feel free to step up and join in.

Closed group   **Open group**

Manage Your Energy

Conferences and multi-hour events require strategic energy management. Since extraverts are energized by being around other people, they are in their sweet spot, often opting for full-on engagement from breakfast to nightcap.

Introverts, on the other hand, may want to be more selective for when they are "on" and when they are recharging. Feel free to excuse yourself from the group that's going to happy hour before dinner, or if you need a few minutes to recharge after lunch, before the afternoon sessions start. Most important, you never need to apologize for opting out of an activity. Each person finds their center and their energy in their own way. Be true to yourself.

Be Memorable

If you're attending an event with a speaker, ask a question during the Q&A session. Make sure it's a good question—to the point and with no meandering preamble. If you've done your homework in advance, you will have a good sense of the speaker's writing and her work. If you can't read her books, at least read a few of the reviews.

The more concise the question, the more memorable you will be. The speaker will thank you as well. Asking a concise, relevant question will etch you in the mind of the speaker as well as many of the like-minded people in the audience. After you've asked a good question in a public forum, do not be surprised if several people come to you afterward and pick up the conversation where the question left off. It has happened to me on many occasions.

Another strategy is to arrive at a speaker's session ten to fifteen minutes before it is scheduled to begin. A good speaker will arrive early to set up, allowing time in case anything goes wrong. If the setup goes well, they then have a few minutes to spare. This is a good time to chat one-on-one and ask some questions.

Brad, a good friend, tells me of the time he arrived early at a conference session featuring the chief technology officer (CTO) of Target Stores. After his brief "pre-talk" conversation with the CTO, Brad then sat in the front row. Brad recounts, with glee, how the CTO talked almost directly to him for the entire presentation, making eye contact and asking if he had questions when he looked confused. It was like a two-person discussion in a room full of onlookers. After the event, the CTO remembered Brad and was willing to connect with him on LinkedIn.

In addition to engaging with speakers before and after their talks, show empathy and ask interesting questions in all your conversations. People long to be heard. Asking good questions shows interest and respect, and goes a long way toward helping people feel heard.

Remember People's Names[*]

Remember people's names. It is a sign of respect for them as a fellow human being. Strive to remember their name because your goal is to build a mutually beneficial relationship with them, and knowing their name is a crucial first step in that process. Remember their name because it forms a cornerstone in your memory for all the other tidbits and facts you will remember about them.

The first step in remembering people's names is to decide that you will make the effort to remember names. Lest you think that a daunting task, remember the wonderful quote by astronaut Jim Lovell: "From now on we live in a world where man has walked on the moon. It's not a miracle; we just decided to go."[48] Commit to making the effort. Decide that you will remember people's names. It gets easier the more you try.

There is a wealth of resources online for improving your memory, particularly improving your ability to remember people's names. Here are a few of my personal tried-and-true techniques for remembering the names of people I meet:

---

[*] One reason that I strongly advocate advanced preparation when meeting with people is that it frees my mind during the meeting to dance in the moment. Instead of being distracted trying to conjure what I might say next, my preparation developing questions and deciding what I will say about myself means that I have more mental capacity to absorb their name and other details they are sharing with me as we talk.

- When I first meet someone, I am hyper-alert for their name so that I don't miss it the first time they offer it.

- If their name is unfamiliar to me, I have a two-fold challenge: I first have to file their unfamiliar name away in the memory banks that hold names, and then I have to associate that name with the person I am talking to.* This takes a little extra effort. I will compliment them on the uniqueness of their name (to me) and ask them to repeat it—often more than once—while I commit it to memory. I make no apologies for the fact that I want to remember their name.

- I assume that people have the same desire to remember my name as I do theirs. I enunciate my name clearly, looking at them directly as I speak it. If I'm not sure they got it, I don't hesitate to repeat it.

- I draw from the memory experts and use their technique of associating the person and/or their name with someone or something with which I am already familiar. Perhaps they look like my uncle, or their name rhymes with one of my favorite words. It doesn't matter what the association is, just that I have associated them and their name with something else already in my brain.

- I mull over their name as I am conversing. Keeping their name top of mind helps me move it from short-term to long-term memory.

- I use their name periodically during the conversation and especially when signing off. "Bob, it's been a pleasure meeting you..." Be careful not to overuse their name or you will sound like a huckster trying to sell them a new car.

---

* This is how memory works. It's as if our brain holds a database of familiar names. When we meet someone whose name matches one we have heard before, all we have to do is associate this person with that familiar name. But when we meet someone with an unfamiliar name, we first have to create a record in our "names" database for that new name. That takes some effort. Once the name is registered in our brain, then we can associate it with this person. This often takes time.

Overcoming Forgetfulness

What do you do if the person has told you their name but it failed to lodge in your memory? You know the feeling. You have this moment of embarrassing self-awareness when you realize that you should know their name and cannot think of what it is. It's as if their name evaporated into thin air. You slip into emergency recovery mode, trying desperately to recall their name while their voice—and the substance of what they are saying—fades into the background like the voices of the adults in the old Peanuts cartoons.[49]

Again, I make no apologies for my desire to remember their name. In this case, I apologize profusely for my mental slip-up and ask them to repeat their name one more time. A little self-deprecation helps—as does my genuine desire to remember their name.

After: Follow Up

As with any networking encounter, follow-up is essential to building good relationships. Large events can be overwhelming, with names and dates and points of remembrance spilling out of your head, not to mention the business cards spilling out of your pockets. Capture the essence of these tidbits in a notebook or on a piece of paper as quickly as possible. I sometimes even make a few quick notes to myself during a bio break. When I get back to my office, I transfer the information from my scribbles, along with the information on the business cards, to the appropriate entry in my address book or a note in Evernote.

Once the key information has been recorded for posterity, proceed with the rest of your follow-up routines:

- Send email or handwritten notes.
- Pass on articles or information.
- Make introductions.
- Follow up monthly, quarterly, or annually.

Chapter 20

Job Searching and Networking

Our life's work, and the meaning we derive from it, is much too important to delegate to "the company" to manage.

Ruben Rodriguez[50]

This is not a book about searching for a job per se. There is no shortage of fantastic resources in that regard. Some of my favorites include anything by Nick Corcodilos at "Ask The Headhunter,"[51] the invaluable audio interview series from Mark Horstman and Michael Auzenne at "Manager Tools,"[52] and the robust body of work by Liz Ryan at "The Human Workplace."[53]

This is, however, a book about networking. And since every career resource in the world—including this one—will tell you that networking is an important aspect of finding a job, a few words are in order.

First and foremost, a few pitfalls to avoid. Most important, when you find yourself scouting for new job opportunities, you can't just ask the people in your network if they have a job for you. As I mentioned above, that's not networking; it's groveling. Networking is about sharing who you know and what you know to help people be successful, not asking for something as significant as a job.

Nor is it worthwhile to blast an email out to your network asking them to pass your résumé along to anyone they might know who is hiring. Same thing: net-groveling. I would recommend these tactics if they worked, but in general they don't. Most people don't have a job to offer and they rarely know anyone who does. While networking does include the exchange of favors and information, asking for something people don't have—especially when they know how important it is to you—just makes them feel bad that they can't be more helpful.

The good news is that there are much better ways to discover job opportunities. The essence of my job-search strategy stems from three fundamental beliefs about successful careers:

> *Rule #1: If you're looking for an opportunity, you're looking for a person.*
>
> *Rule #2: Seek first to add value.*
>
> *Rule #3: The best job description is the one you write yourself.*

The Allure of Job Postings

When we find ourselves searching for our next career opportunity, our first inclination is to hit the job boards. Am I right? We spend a few hours clicking our way through LinkedIn's job listings, CareerBuilder, Indeed.com, or some company-specific site. In our dream scenario we stumble upon the perfect job posting, apply online, ace the phone interview (because we are such a perfect fit for the job), are brought in for face-to-face interviews, receive an offer, and are hired. While this is the general sequence of events for most people who get hired, people have deeply misguided assumptions about the process. Networking to the rescue.

What's wrong with this picture? Let's stop and explore what we know and, more important, what we don't know when we see a job posting online. Here's what we know:

- The company that is hiring is in a good place. They are hiring employees, not letting people go. There is enough demand that they have decided to add another member to the team.
- There is a manager somewhere in the company who is overwhelmed and in pain. She has enough work for at least

one additional person. We know this because if she didn't have enough work for an additional person, then her manager would encourage her to "wait until she could justify the extra headcount" or try to redistribute the work without bringing on another person.

- The organization has a budget for another employee.
- The hiring manager has gone through the usually arduous process of getting approval to hire someone. This is no small feat, especially in large organizations.

Here's what we *don't know:*

- We don't know much about the job itself.
- We don't know what the hiring manager really needs.
- We don't know how your unique combination of skills and experience might bring more to the role than the hiring manager ever imagined.
- We don't know what other needs there might be elsewhere in the company.

Given that we have the posted job description, how is it that we don't really know anything about the job itself? Because we have a job description, we *think* we know what they are looking for. However, in my experience there is only about a 50 percent correlation between what the hiring manager needs and what the job description indicates. There are two reasons for this:

First, most job descriptions are written under duress. Did I mention that hiring managers are usually overwhelmed? After all, if they aren't drowning in work, they have a hard time justifying a new position to their boss(es).

To make matters worse, the hiring manager may not have even written the job description you just stumbled upon. Often an assistant or partner from human resources will write the job description and post it in all the right places. To do so, they typically consult with the hiring manager and then copy and paste sections from other job descriptions to create something that bears some resemblance to what they think the hiring manager has asked for.

The second reason there is such a low correlation between what the hiring manager needs and what the job posting describes is that hiring managers don't know what they truly need. In most cases, they know what they *think* they need, but they haven't met you yet. They have yet to see what you can see through the lens of your experience and accumulated skills. Most of the time, hiring managers don't fully understand what they need until they have met the ideal candidate, at which point they realize that they need more of what the ideal candidate can offer and less of what they wrote in the job description. It happens almost every time.

Finally, they likely have other needs in the company or even elsewhere on the hiring manager's team. A good hiring manager will be on the lookout for talent for the entire company, not just for their team. Until you have an opportunity to talk with the hiring manager, you don't know where you might best fit within the organization.

Enter Networking

If you're looking for an opportunity, you're looking for a person. Once you find a job posting that looks even remotely interesting—at a company in which you think you might want to work—your next step is to use your network to "burrow your way into the organization." Reach out to your first- and second-degree network connections in the company. Find out what it's like to work there, what kinds of work they do, and what kinds of people succeed there. Your goal is to formulate what you think they need and what your work might look like. Request introductions and informational interviews that will eventually connect you with the hiring manager.

Or vice versa. Instead of searching for job postings, search for organizations in which you would like to work. Use your network to burrow your way into the company and find out what they need. It's likely that what they need hasn't even made its way to a job posting yet. If you can find someone who as a need, and then show that you can add more value than what it would cost them to pay you, there's a good chance that a position can be created (if one doesn't already exist) and that a job offer will follow.

Seek First to Add Value

The focus of your exploration is to learn how you might leverage your skills, experience, and network in a way that the company finds valuable. Or, in the language of networking, your goal is to leverage who and what you know to help someone be successful.

You and only you are fully aware of what you bring to the table. It is up to you to translate your potential contributions into value that the company needs. Don't hold your breath hoping for a job offer. Figure out what problems and challenges the hiring manager is facing—don't take their word for it. Use your unique perspective to see things that they haven't seen yet. Convince yourself and the hiring manager that you can solve their problems and generate value. If you cannot generate enough value to cover the cost of your employment, then there is no way the company can justify bringing you on board.[54]

Write Your Own Job Description

The best job description is the one you write yourself. After all, who knows better what you have to offer, what you can do, what you are working on in the medium and long term, and what you might want to do next? When you find yourself working at the intersection of who you are, what you are good at, and what the company needs, you are in your sweet spot. Getting there is not as hard as you might think.

If you're already working inside the company, either as a contractor or a full-time employee, then you have it made. Use your insider view to find or create necessary work that is uniquely suited to you. Talk to your boss, your peers, and your boss's peers to find out what people are working on. Using your own skills and interests as a lens, figure out what the organization needs. Work with your manager to modify your job description to better suit what you can do vis-à-vis what they need.

Or work with other managers elsewhere in the company to create or modify a position for you.

It can be more difficult to write your own job description if you are interviewing for a position from outside the company. It is diffi-cult—but still quite possible—to customize a job description so that it is well-suited to your sweet spot. Imagine yourself in the role. Focus on what they need and how you might be helpful. The hiring manager, along with the entire interview team, will begin to follow your lead, imagining you in the role.

I have found that during the interview process, the surest way to imagine yourself immersed in the role is to simply adopt the mindset that you are putting together a 90-day plan *as if you already have the job.* Ask yourself some of the key 90-day planning questions:[*]

- What are some of the overall goals and objectives that you would expect me to accomplish during my first 90 days?

- What are two or three "quick wins" that would jump-start this role?

- What would I need to learn?

- Who would I need to meet?

- What would be some of my key deliverables?

You get the idea. Everyone, yourself included, will begin to see you already in the position. The questions you ask will clarify the work that needs to be done, and the potential solutions you propose will show how you can add value. This is how job descriptions get rewritten. While the hiring manager may not rewrite the job description before extending a job offer, it is quite common to have that job description rewritten for you—or by you—by the time you reach your six-month anniversary with the company.

Writing your own job description happens more often than you might think. It is made possible by building a strong network in your organization and then relentlessly looking for ways to add value based

---

[*] A handy "Individual Jump-Start Worksheet" is available at heatherhollick.com/individual-jump-start.

on who and what you know. Contract opportunities can be a godsend here. You are given full access to a company and a finite window to network and identify ways to add value. If you play your cards right — and leverage your network well — you can create amazing opportunities for yourself.

Chapter 21

Informational Interviews

A ship in harbor is safe, but that is not what ships are built for.

Unknown*

How do you choose the next direction for your career? Would you like to be more visible in your company? Or do you think you want to work for another company? Perhaps you're thinking about writing a book, or starting a podcast, and would like to talk to someone who has done it before.

An informational interview involves talking with people who are already doing what you want to do. The purpose of the interview is to learn, to understand, and to begin to build a network of contacts in that field. In my speaking and client engagements, I frequently find myself recommending informational interviews. They are a full, natural extension of good networking and are built upon all the principles that we have espoused thus far. Unfortunately, informational interviews are often misunderstood and underused as a career-management tool.

When to Use Informational Interviews

As the name implies, informational interviews are a great way to gather information, usually from someone who has firsthand knowledge, especially about ideas or a field of work that is new to you. Informational

---

* In my first year out of college I taught high-school math and physics. On the wall I hung this quote as a motivational poster. According to Quote Investigator, it is attributed to various sources, including a U.S. Navy Rear Admiral and Albert Einstein.

interviews are also a great way to explore new career directions, expand your visibility in your organization, find a mentor, deepen your understanding of a company, fashion new opportunities, and prepare for a job interview. I am sure that you can think of other situations where they would be helpful. We'll explore many of these possibilities in the remainder of the book.

Exploring and Expanding Career Options

There are many times in our lives when we decide that our careers need a definite shift in direction. For me, one of those times — turning 40 — led me to pursue an MBA from the Haas School at UC Berkeley. As graduation approached, it seemed like the perfect time to make a career pivot. But what to do next?

Decades earlier, my background in mathematics and the sciences had led me down the path of least resistance into information technology. This time I wanted to be more deliberate in my career choice. I narrowed my interests down to three distinct post-MBA career trajectories. I have always been fascinated by logistics and complex supply-chain systems. But then again, I have natural gifts as a leader, and complex organizational systems fascinated me as well. Moreover, it seemed like half of my classmates were product managers or were planning to pursue product management after graduation. As that seemed to be the de facto career path for MBAs, I figured that I had better explore that avenue as well.

So, in my final semester of school, while attending classes part time and working full time, I seized the moment and reached out to more than twenty accomplished people in supply-chain management, human resources, and product management. Over the course of six months I conducted twenty-four informational interviews with twenty-four wise and generous souls. Their insights and encouragement still echo to this day. I ended up moving from IT leadership into human resources and leadership development.* I have never looked back.

---

* Although if the tech bubble had not been about to burst, prompting a sudden hiring freeze at Cisco, I might have ended up working in supply-chain management. Fate can be funny that way.

Networking at Work

Building relationships inside your company or organization is so important to job and career success that the entire final section of this book is dedicated to the topic. For now, suffice it to say that informational interviews are an ideal way to learn who the players are and to gain insights into what's happening elsewhere in the company. Besides helping you perform better in your role, these kinds of insights will help you understand how careers work at your company and give you essential knowledge to help you navigate your career there.

For example, within the first ninety days in a new role, I recommend that you conduct informational interviews with a wide variety of stakeholders and constituents, including your peers, your manager's peers, and vendors. If you manage projects, develop products, or work in a support function, then you also have a broad list of key stakeholders whom you support, interact with, and influence. These people are all excellent candidates for informational interviews. Understand their role in the company, what they are working on, their drivers, and their constraints. Use this information to shape the work that you do and the results you deliver.

Mentors and Job Searching

Informational interviews are a great way to find mentors and, as we discussed in Chapter 20, are an integral part of any job search strategy. We'll come back to mentors and mentoring in the next chapter.

Getting the Interview

The best way to get an informational interview is simply to ask. I have been on both the giving and receiving ends of dozens of informational interviews. In my experience, people are happy to meet with you if you approach them with reverence and respect. People enjoy being helpful, and they feel good when given the opportunity to talk about something they know well.

- Don't be afraid to ask. It's okay to ask for help.

- Ask friends and colleagues to make a warm introduction, if possible.
- Use LinkedIn to find candidates.
- Have a purpose for your request.

Do's and Don'ts

Getting on someone's calendar for an informational interview is a good first step — but once it's scheduled, you need to take steps to make sure you come off as professional as possible. Here are a few suggestions for scheduling and conducting successful informational interviews:

- Approach the interview like a dress rehearsal for a job interview. However, don't ask for a job. The point is to learn something.
- Avoid any appearances of net-groveling. You may be looking for a job, but that is not the point of an informational interview. Do not send your résumé — unless asked for it — or use any language that implies you are looking for a job. Don't abuse the person's willingness to be helpful.
- Be prepared with an arsenal of good questions. You won't get to all of them. That's okay.
- Do your homework. Be prepared with a good understanding of the experience, background, and responsibilities of the person you are meeting. Don't ask questions that you could have found the answers to in advance with the help of Google, LinkedIn, or company websites.
- Honor people's time. Request thirty to forty-five minutes — no more than an hour — then stick to it. If the interview is running beyond the requested time, avoid the temptation to keep talking. Ask if it would be better to schedule a follow-up conversation.
- Don't talk too much. Be prepared to answer a few questions about yourself, but your principal role is to ask questions of them.

- Be a good networker. Find out what they are working on and look for ways to be helpful.

What to Ask

There is no end to the list of great questions you could ask in an informational interview. Your list will depend on the person you are interviewing and your objectives for the interview.

Here are a few sample questions that might stimulate your thinking[55]:

1. Which of your accomplishments or challenges were the most helpful for your career?

2. Which of your decisions have had the most impact on your career?

3. What are the nuances to being successful in this company? In this industry?

4. Who are the important people to know in this company? In this industry? Why?

5. What would you do differently if you were starting your career over?

6. What would you do if you were in my situation right now?

7. What problems have you solved? How?

8. What are your drivers?

9. What are your constraints?

10. How have you increased revenues, profits?

11. How have you improved processes?

12. How have you demonstrated creativity, innovation?

13. How have you reduced costs?

As with all networking encounters, look for ways to reciprocate and be helpful in return. A quid pro quo is not expected, but you should always be asking yourself, "What is this person working on? Who do I know and what do I know that could help them be successful?"

Chapter 22

Finding and Leveraging Mentors and Coaches

*If I have seen further than others,
it is by standing upon the shoulders of giants.*

Isaac Newton

Why, you might ask, are we talking about mentors and mentoring in a book about networking? Three reasons: because the spirit of mentoring is simply an extension of the spirit of good networking; because success is nuanced and you need all the help and insights you can get; and because being a mentor is a powerful way to share who and what you know with others. Let's explore these reasons more deeply.

First, we're talking about mentors and mentoring in a book on networking because the give and take of mentoring—especially the privilege of being a mentor—is just an advanced form of good networking. To be a mentor is simply to share who and what you know in a way that helps other people be successful. Sound familiar? Mentoring takes to the next level "the constant exchange of favors and information" that defines networking.

Similarly, being under the tutelage of a good mentor is to be on the receiving end of a relationship with a master networker, all the while leveraging your own knowledge and network to help your mentor be successful. It's a mutually beneficial relationship and networking in its purest form. Success is a team sport. We know we need help, but we often go looking in all the wrong places. Mentors help us find that team.

Second, we're talking about mentors and mentoring because this is a book about careers and professional success. Despite what you see on the best-seller list—or your Facebook timeline—success is nuanced and often elusive. I've come to believe that business biographies and popular leadership profiles do more harm than good. They are pop-culture pablum. The biographies of the "mega-successful" lead us to believe that there are silver bullets to success. Just "put fun first"[56] and we'll be as rich as Richard Branson, or "lead from our gut"[57] and we'll be as successful as Jack Welch. Oh, if only that were true.

The truth is more nuanced. The building blocks of success are subtle and situational. The things we need to know and learn vary widely across organizations, industries, markets, and time. Most of all, success is uniquely personal. The capabilities and characteristics that lead to our success accumulate incrementally from where *we* are now and lead to what *we* are ready for next. While I'm all for fun, and I trust my gut more than most, we need more than that to be successful. We need to learn from those who came before us.

Finally, we are talking about mentoring in a book about networking because mentoring is a way for you to scale your impact. By the second half of your career, you have more skills and experience than any one employer can leverage. There are an almost infinite number of things that you could do that leverage who you are and what you have to offer in exchange for a livelihood and some personal satisfaction. Mentoring others allows you to tap into more of who you are and what you have to offer. Being a mentor can be an enriching and satisfying experience.

Learning From Mentors

When I speak about careers, I often ask for a show of hands of people who currently have a mentor. A sprinkling of hands inch up timidly, as if they were gently being raised by a marionettist. Then I ask, "How many people *wish* they had a mentor?" and nearly every hand in the room shoots straight up. Everyone craves a mentor. I think it's partly how we're wired as humans. We are, after all, social creatures. And yet very few people connect meaningfully with a mentor, and fewer still experience ongoing mentor-mentee relationships that help their careers in a meaningful way.

In bygone eras you started your career at the bottom of an organization and set your sights on the corner office. If you were good—and a bit lucky—a company veteran tapped you on the shoulder and took you under their wing. They showed you the ropes. They introduced you to the right people. They taught you how to lead, and they made sure that you got what you needed to be successful. We reverently called these people our "mentors." This kind of "grooming" doesn't happen much anymore.

What's changed? We're still ambitious. We're still eager to learn, to be successful, and to connect with the right people. We still crave that tap on the shoulder from someone who will show us the ropes. But the taps don't come as often these days, and they rarely come unsolicited.

In our hunger for growth, progress, and success, we have clung to a simplistic view of a mentor and an outdated desire for someone who will spot our potential, take us under their wing, and co-pilot our careers. We pine for a relationship with a wise and mature mentor who meets with us once or twice a month over a long period of time and imparts wisdom like a college professor working through a syllabus.

It doesn't work that way anymore—if it ever did. Modern business is much more complex than ever, and organizations are more fragmented now. To be successful in this modern era requires a wider range of experiences, capabilities, and connections than any one person can teach you.

Against this backdrop of complex companies and their mystifying cultures, our career aspirations become amorphous. It's hard to dream about what we want when the path to getting there is so unclear. The key to succeeding in this complicated world is to understand what we really want and truly need.

In essence, what we *want* is to develop and grow as human beings and progress in our careers as professionals. What we *need* is a little help along the way. It helps to realize that we are all free agents now and that no one person or program can give us everything we want and need.

Self-Service Career Development

How do we take our leadership and career development into our own hands? We can look at how organizations have developed leaders over the last several decades for clues on how to get what we need.

First, a leadership-development industry emerged in the second half of the twentieth century. Then, over the last few decades, significant changes in the leadership-development industry occurred. While there has long been a market for workshops, classes, business degrees, and in-house leadership-development programs, the demand for executive and professional coaching has markedly increased over the last several years. What's going on? Why is everyone suddenly interested in working with a coach?

In response to the changing dynamics in our ever-leaner organizations, a propitious division of labor has emerged in the development of leaders. Some—but not all—of what we need in the areas of professional and leadership development has been outsourced to accomplished, professional coaches. Understanding this division will help us understand the role of mentors as well.

It turns out that to be fully alive and to grow as a leader, we need the kind of learning and growth emanating from three distinct sources: self-help, coaches, and mentors.

Self Help: Fundamental and Universal

The table stakes of what we need to be successful in the business world is a basic understanding of how to function on teams and in organizations. We need fundamental skills that are universal and applicable to many levels and organizations, such as the basic skills of being a good employee, manager, or leader. This category includes basic competencies in such areas as:

- Management of your time and energy;[58]
- Task management and getting things done;[59]
- The ability to communicate with many personality types and various audiences;

- Basic management skills, such as hiring, firing, delegation, and performance management;*
- Leadership skills beyond those of a first-level manager.[60]

In all these areas you are most effectively and economically served by working at your own pace with the help of books, websites, workshops, and classes. I have mentioned just a few in the footnotes and endnotes.

Coaching: Contextual and Personal

As you master the fundamentals, the next level of growth is both contextual and personal. It's contextual in the sense that no book or self-help workshop could adequately address your unique personality or relate to your specific boss, team, or culture—in short, your context. In this case, you need someone who has seen these situations before, to offer a different or fresh perspective, help you understand your environment, and plot a path of growth.

In addition, growth is often personal. You have blind spots. You may not know as much as you think you know.[61] You also have misconceptions, things that you take to be true that are not. As the old saying goes, it's not what we don't know that gets us into trouble. It's what we know for sure that just isn't so.

Professional growth also requires a significant degree of self-discovery. To some degree, we're all stuck in our own reality, seeing the world through our own lenses, believing what our thoughts tell us to be true. We have attitudes, behaviors, and beliefs that may have served us well in the past but are now holding us back. A coach can help you break through to a new level of self-awareness.

There is also a powerful efficacy to working with a coach. Sure, you can try to work out your challenges on your own. But excessive

---

* The abundance of resources offered by "Manager Tools" are second to none. They focus on management and communication skills with an eye towards first-time and front-line managers. In addition to invaluable free podcasts, they offer online resources and in-person workshops rich with opportunities for personal and experiential learning. Explore all that they have to offer at **manager-tools.com**.

attachment to self-help results in struggling with problems that could be quickly solved with the help of a professional coach.[62]

For all these reasons, you will periodically want to work with a professional or executive coach during your career. A coach is a trained and experienced leadership-development expert whose focus is to help you be successful in business. Drawing upon research, training, experience, and their own natural gifts, good coaches help you grow both personally and professionally. They provide an outside perspective and insights garnered across diverse careers and experiences. They challenge you to see your blind spots. They explore with you, so you can better articulate your values and keep them in focus. A good coach will help you build the right team, develop your ability to influence, bolster your confidence, strengthen your presence, better manage your time, achieve work-life balance, and learn how to manage a challenging situation or a difficult boss. Give yourself a few intense periods in your professional life in which you work with a good coach. It will help you get unstuck, get clear, and get ahead.

Mentors: Nuanced and Relational

Beyond what you can achieve on your own and with a good coach, a workshop or a coach can't help you with certain key areas of success. Some of what we need is specific to our organization, our culture, or our market. There are things you need to know that only an insider knows.

Most important, regardless of how good your individual performance is, success ultimately comes down to relationships. By now you know enough to build a broad array of mutually beneficial relationships. But to truly supercharge your career, you need connections and introductions to the movers and the shakers in your company, in your town, or in your industry.

This is where mentors come in. While a coach can help you be successful in business, a mentor can help you be successful in *your* business, in *your* organization, or in *your* industry. A good mentor knows the nuances of your industry and has honed their instincts over the years. They will have the tacit knowledge that often marks the difference between being mediocre and being remarkable. The right mentors have inside information that a coach could never know, and can pass along the knowledge and wisdom that come only from a lifetime of observations and experience.

As I've been saying all along, much success results from building and leveraging the right relationships (this is a book about networking, after all). While a coach may help you develop your basic networking skills, she doesn't necessarily know *who* you need to know. She doesn't know the key players in your company or in your industry. And even if your coach *did* know the people you need to know, she can't make the introductions—you need an insider to do that. You need a mentor.

The key to a good introduction is timing. A mentor not only can make introductions to important people but can also groom you to be ready to meet them. I beg you not to undervalue this step. Remember that all relationships need to be mutually beneficial. Introductions—especially with movers and shakers—work best when both parties are ready to meet. An ideal question for a mentor is, "Who do I need to know in this company?" The follow-up question is, "What do *I* need to know *before* I meet them?" Or better yet, "Where do I need to be professionally in order to be able to get—and offer—the most out of a potential relationship?"

While working with a mentor feels personal, don't make the mistake of burdening a mentor with the things that you could have learned on your own or with the help of a coach. This is one of the biggest mistakes that people make when looking for a mentor. Don't expect a mentor to do what you could have achieved through some other means.

Drive your own growth and your own career. Hire a coach to understand your situation, to work on yourself, and to shine light on your blind spots. And concurrently with all of the above, seek out and build relationships with mentors who can help you with the insights and the connections you need to be successful in your business. It's the perfect division of labor. You want mentors as well as a coach, all operating on a rich bed of self-awareness and amplified by your efforts to learn and grow on your own.

How To Find a Mentor

People who crave the life- and career-enhancing power of a great mentoring relationship often get ahead of themselves. They make the mistake of setting out too quickly in search of a mentor before they are ready. Do your homework before you even begin to look for people who could serve as mentors in your life. There are prerequisites. You have to be ready, and you have to be willing to do the work.

Self-Awareness

First, to be ready to work with a mentor, be willing to work on yourself. You have to know yourself. Start by enhancing your awareness of who you are. What's important to you? What interests you? What are some of your key values? Where are you in your career? Are you willing to work fifty to sixty hours per week? To travel? To relocate? In what environments do you work best? How do you communicate?

Second, what are you good at? What are your key strengths? What are your credentials and degrees? What is your experience? What have you been doing, especially lately? What skills have you been developing? What have you learned?

Related to your personal strengths is the strength of your network. Who do you know? How connected are you? Could you tap into your network for information or resources if the need arose? What is your reputation? How are you known?

And finally, self-awareness includes a keen sense of what you want and need to learn next. What are you working on? What are you ready for? How do you want to be known?

Self-awareness is hard work. But what are the alternatives? If you want to do your best work—and be your best self—then not being self-aware is not an option. To thrive, you must have a confident sense of who you are, a keen sense of who you want to be, a clear sense of what you are ready for, and a passion for what you want to learn.

Ready and Willing to Work Hard

The second prerequisite for working effectively with a mentor is to be willing to work hard. A mentor is much more likely to want to work with you if you are hungry to learn. Ambition is stimulating and contagious.

Think about this from the mentor's perspective. You will be asking them to give their time, reveal some of their insights, and tap into their network. What's in it for them? What they will find rewarding is the satisfaction of helping someone along the path of their career, of seeing someone blossom.

Don't expect forever. Mentor-mentee relationships are rarely perpetual. They are often rhythmic, with periods of intense working together followed by more reflective periods in which the learnings take root (the same applies to coaching). This is how learning works. It is also how long-term relationships can remain healthy and mutually beneficial.

Don't limit yourself to one mentor. When you know yourself, what you are ready for, and what you want to work on, you could have multiple mentors at once, each helping you in a specific area.

Reach Out

With your prerequisites well in hand and a healthy mindset of what to expect from a mentor, you are ready to look for people who can help you learn what you crave to learn. Look for people who are looking for you.[63] They're all around you—people who know you and can see your potential. Study people you admire and figure out why you admire them so much.

When you find interesting people, develop a strategy to engage with them. For goodness' sake, don't send an email up front to someone who doesn't know you and ask them to be your mentor. Follow their work. Navigate your network. Let it be known in your network that there are people you would love to meet; ask for favors and help to work your way toward an eventual introduction.

When you are ready to reach out, don't ask the person to be your mentor initially, if ever. Instead, ask for thirty minutes of their time for an informational interview. Tell them (honestly) that you admire them and would like to learn from them.

When You Meet

When you finally get a chance to meet with a potential mentor, follow all the guidelines of informational interviews: do your homework, let them do most of the talking, respect their time, and so forth. Ask good questions.

What differentiates a mentoring relationship from general informational interviews is that in the former, it's all about asking targeted questions that get at the subtle, nuanced elements of their success. Here are some questions that might get you started:

1. How did you learn to navigate the company culture?
2. What are the nuances of success in this organization/industry?
3. What do you know now that you wish you'd known when you were starting out?
4. Who are the people you need to know to be successful in this organization/industry?
5. What do you need to do to be ready to meet them?
6. When the time is right, will you introduce me?

Wrap up with the granddaddy of all mentor questions: "What would you do if you were in my situation?" Note the specific wording of this question. Don't ask, "What should I do?" Ask them what they would do in your situation. By phrasing the question this way, you're not asking for advice per se (giving advice is difficult for many people). Instead, you are asking them to see you for who you are and then reflect on what they would do in the same situation.

Then keep in touch. Schedule ongoing meetings with this mentor for as long as the relationship seems mutually beneficial. Be sure to reciprocate in any way that you can. Be a good networker. You know people and things that could help them be successful as well. Success is a team sport.

It Goes Both Ways

Finally, a key to having great mentors is to strive to always be a mentor as well. It's as important to give as it is to receive. Constantly be on the lookout for potential and undeveloped talent. When you see it, invite them to meet with you and do what you can to help them on their way. Don't wait to be asked. Mentoring goes both ways.

Summary

Mentoring takes on different roles as people move through their careers. When you're young, you will primarily be looking to be on the receiving end of a mentor-mentee relationship.[*] As you gain experience and mature in wisdom, you will want to mentor others as much as you receive the gifts of a mentor. And as you round out your career, the pendulum shifts more fully to the giving side as you share your insights and your connections with younger, ambitious professionals.

Regardless of whether you are on the giving or receiving end of a mentorship, the most potent way to grow both personally and professionally over your career is to take a three-pronged approach that strategically leverages a combination of leadership-development books, classes, workshops, and programs; sprints with a professional coach; and relationships with an array of carefully selected mentors. Self-help, coaching, and mentoring, both giving and receiving. Can you do it?

---

[*] Although "reverse mentoring" is on the rise, in which older executives are paired with younger employees to learn about current attitudes, trends, and such topics as technology and social media.

Part IV
Networking At Work

Chapter 23

Inside Networking

If a company wants to outstrip its competitors, it needs to influence not only how people work but also how they work together.

Charles Duhigg[64]

One of the greatest misconceptions about networking is that its primary, if not sole, purpose is to help you find a job. Managers and leaders with this misconception fear that employees who network are a flight risk to the company. More than one company where I have worked has gone so far as to block access to LinkedIn at the corporate firewall.

Sure, networking is a key component of finding your next opportunity. Again, if you're looking for an opportunity, you're looking for a person. But by now I hope you can see that networking is so much more than a path to finding a job. Networking is a mindset for how we interact with one another. It's a way of embracing the world—with a spirit of community, interconnectedness, and helpfulness.

In this final section of the book, we will explore not only how the networking mindset is essential for a successful career, but also how building a strong web of professional relationships *inside your organization* is critical to your individual performance in your role and, most likely, to your company's long-term performance. We will see that our definition of networking—and its inherent spirit of helpfulness—is synonymous with teamwork and collaboration. Further, teams of employees who are actively freshening and strengthening links with one another create a vibrant organization infused with energy and enthusiasm, where people enjoy working.

Companies Win Too

Not only is individual networking essential to personal career success, but it is also becoming a differentiator for the long-term success of many companies. Researchers are finding that well-networked organizations outperform their poorly networked counterparts. IBM found that high-performing organizations are 57 percent more likely than other companies to provide their global teams with collaborative and social-networking tools.[65] Similarly, McKinsey & Company found that well-networked organizations delivered higher market share and profits than less-networked companies delivered.[66]

Finally, a seminal study published in the *MIT Management Review* in 2011 shows that a well-networked organization is the latest evolution in organizational structure and talent management. In "Building a Well-Networked Organization," the authors argue, "Senior executives would do well to give as much thought to the design, development, and facilitation of networks as they historically have given to organizational structure and reporting relationships."[67]

Bringing It Inside

If you take everything we have learned so far about networking and begin to practice it in your organization, you will see that it all fits perfectly. With "inside networking," all the same insights, guidelines, and recommendations for building and nurturing a network of professional relationships apply equally to relationships with colleagues. Upon bringing the networking mindset into your organization, you will start to see your job — and your company — differently. You will deliver results more effectively, and you will increase the value that you add to the organization. You might even start to experience a new spring in your step.

These networking methods apply equally well in organizations of all natures and sizes, in the public and private sectors, in for-profit and non-profit organizations, and everything in between. Further, building and leveraging a powerful network inside these complex environments is not optional for you or your company. Not only is networking inside your organization a powerful amplifier for your career, but it is becoming an imperative for organizations to thrive.

Being a well-networked employee is about creating, freshening, and strengthening links. And it's about understanding what other people are working on and then leveraging who and what you know to help them be successful. Beyond just your career, these behaviors and relationships are becoming critical to the success of your team and the long-term viability of your company.

Chapter 24

The Modern Organization

Extensive informal networks are so important that if they do not exist, creating them has to be the focus of activity early in a major leadership initiative.

John P. Kotter[68]

To understand how networking amplifies careers, we have to understand a few things about the current state of the modern organization. Like our broader culture, organizations—including their structure and composition—evolve over time. Just as the general global population is moving from low-density rural living to higher-density suburban and urban lifestyles, the range of organizations from which we earn our livings is expanding from small, local businesses to large, complex, multi-regional, and global entities.

For centuries, the organizations in which people worked to earn a livelihood were quite small: family farms, small shops, and sole proprietorships. Organizations were simple. Leadership and power flowed unquestionably from a single source, usually the patriarch or the shop owner. To be successful you did what the owner (or your father) told you to do.

Things began to change rapidly with the advent of industrialization. The twentieth century saw the emergence of complex, hierarchical organizational structures. The labor of hundreds—and then thousands—of people was harnessed within the boundaries of single organizations. Think of General Motors, which was distinguished as the world's largest corporation for many years. In these early days of large organizations, a small cadre of leaders, perched high in the organization, held power.* To be successful you kept your head down and played your small part. You followed the process. The organizational and power structures mirrored the assembly lines on the plant floor.

As manual labor began to give way to knowledge work in the late twentieth century, the nature of the organization and how the work was managed began to change as well. We saw the emergence of "matrixed" organizations, an array of complex reporting structures containing a hodgepodge of "solid-line" and "dotted-line"† reports sprinkled around and through the org chart.

At the same time, traditional process-driven workflows (e.g., assembly lines and simple supply chains) were proving inadequate. A large portion of the work in organizations began to get "chunked" into discrete projects, whereby the people needed to complete the work no longer reported up through a single chain of command. Resources might be scattered across teams anywhere in the organization.

To manage this work, the discipline of project management migrated from the realm of construction and civil engineering—where it had been slowly evolving for centuries—to the day-to-day working lives of everyone from software developers to marketing professionals. By the late 1960s the world was ready to formalize and standardize the broader practice of project management. PMI, the Project Management Institute, was founded in 1969 offering training, certifications, and an air of credibility to the emerging profession of project management.

---

* Labor unions emerged as a counterbalance to the plutocratic power structures that managed many of these organizational behemoths.

† The differences between solid-line and dotted-line reporting can be subtle. In both old and new organizations everyone has one person to whom they report directly. This is your solid-line manager, the person who oversees your performance, salary, bonuses, and promotions. However, in modern organizations, where areas of accountability can overlap and intersect, organizational charts may show dotted-line reporting structures in which employees report to multiple people. For example, a senior sales leader may have a solid-line report to his direct boss but also a dotted-line report to the head of marketing. A human-resource leader may have a solid-line report to the head of HR and a dotted-line report to the business he supports.

Tasks were now completed by "resources" (i.e., people) drawn from a literal cross-section of the organization. It would not have been surprising to see people from engineering, marketing, finance, and human resources all contributing to the same project. People reported directly to a manager who had "dotted-line" reporting responsibilities for a wide array of people, functions, or projects within an organization.

In this "projectized" environment, individual responsibilities and accountabilities shifted as work and projects ebbed and flowed. Power, while still primarily defined based on the organizational hierarchy and concentrated at the top, started to diffuse. People found themselves empowered with newfound, often localized authority to make decisions. The influencers, along with the ability to influence decisions and shape the future of projects or initiatives, became detached from the hierarchy of the org chart. Power no longer derived from your rank or position on the org chart.

As organizations continue to evolve in the twenty-first century, they have become more complex, dispersed, distributed, virtual, remote, cross-functional, collaborative, and flat. What were once vertically integrated organizations* are now vast ecosystems often consisting of dozens, if not hundreds, of teams, vendors, and providers. Colleagues and collaborators may report not only to someone in another part of the organization but to a manager in another *company!*

How these complex organizations are led and managed is evolving as well. Top-down hierarchies can't keep up, if they ever could.[69] Power derived from a box on the org chart is being overshadowed by those who garner influence based on their knowledge and their relationships. This is a huge shift. Power now derives from what you know and who you know—as much, if not more, than from your place on the org chart. The modern organizational structure is evolving into a hybrid of a classic organizational chart and a well-networked organization.[70] Jeffrey Pfeffer, a professor at Stanford who has studied power

---

* At one point in its history, the Ford Rouge Plant outside of Dearborn Michigan not only produced its own electricity but was so vertically integrated that they smelted their own iron ore to make their own steel.

and organizational dynamics for decades, points to the heart of the transformation when he says,

> *Simply put, responsibility and authority don't always coincide. As organizations have become more matrixed, with overlapping and dotted-line chains of command, employ more task forces and teams to bring disparate expertise together to solve problems, and face greater demands for speed, the premium for execution is going up. Getting things done under circumstances where you lack direct line authority requires influence and political skills — a knowledge of organizational dynamics — not just technical skills and knowledge.*[71]

This tells us that the modern organization, with its distributed networks of influence and diffused lines of responsibilities, requires extensive collaboration to be successful. Collaboration is more than just cooperation and being nice to your fellow workers. Collaboration is about aligning goals, drivers, and resources while minimizing friction and constraints. That is to say, collaboration is about finding out and understanding what people do and what they're working on, and adjusting accordingly.

While this alignment can and should be modeled at the top and driven by the senior leadership of the organization, it is, in essence, an organic process. The deepest collaboration comes when colleagues engage one another with a spirit of helpfulness, the mindset of networking, and the powerful question, "What are you working on?" Everything else follows.

But this is not a book about modern organizational design or leadership theory. This is about networking, building relationships, and how to navigate a satisfying career. In our few remaining chapters, we'll show how networking as we have defined it becomes synonymous with collaboration once you bring it inside your organization and adapt it for building relationships with colleagues.

Chapter 25

The Elements of Career Success

First, do excellent quality work, which entails hiring and effectively leading outstanding talent. And second, understand the organizational dynamics — how different people perceive things, what their interests are, how to make a persuasive case, and how to get along with people and build effective personal relationships.

Jeffrey Pfeffer[72]

On one hand, success comes to those who work hard to earn it. On the other hand, most successful people will tell you that there's an element of serendipity to a great career. Reality is somewhere in the middle. There is no doubt that you have to be in the right place at the right time with the right skills and the right experience when the right opportunity comes along. Seems like a long shot, right?[73] Not really. If you're reading this, then the odds are most likely already in your favor. Let's look at how networking can increase those odds substantially.

To understand the role of networking in the modern career, it is helpful to shine a spotlight onto the evolving elements that contribute to success in the modern organization. To be successful in most large, complex, corporate environments, you need to get three essential elements right:

- Do *good* work.
- Do the *right* work.
- Be *visible,* especially to the right people.

Obvious, right? So, what does networking have to do with it? As you might have guessed, networking plays a pivotal role in all three areas: doing good work, doing the work that the organization needs (i.e., the right work), and being visible. Let's take a closer look.

Good Work

What does it take to do high-quality work in your field? If your profession falls into the realm of knowledge work, it might take more than you think. Sure, it takes personal talent, training, focused skill development, and maybe even 10,000 hours of practice. But in today's knowledge-based economy it also takes a high degree of collaboration. You cannot be successful in isolation. You need input from others, to be a team player, and to work well with others.

The most successful organizations are alive with the constant exchange of favors and information. It is the perfect arena for a networking mindset. In most cases much of the information you need to do your job resides elsewhere in the organization. The old adage, "No man is an island" was never more true than in the modern workplace. Building relationships across your organization helps you to create a network of knowledge and allies that will contribute directly to the work you do. There will be pockets of information, held by key people, that you will need to be successful. Without them, your work would be mediocre at best. Knowing whom to call and where to find information differentiates you and your team. It will make your best work possible. Building a web of relationships inside your organization is essential for doing good work. The adage, "It's not what you know but who you know" has been upgraded. The modern version reads, "Who you know *IS what you know!*"[74]

In 2011 the *MIT Sloan Management Review* published a seminal study on the effect and extent of networks in organizations by identifying the characteristics of high-performing talent, hidden talent, underutilized talent, and marginalized talent. For high-performing talent, they found that

Early in their employment in organizations, high performers invest in, develop, and renew high-quality network relationships. These personal relationships help them extend their expertise and avoid learning biases by tapping into pockets of knowledge and accessing valuable resources across their networks.[75]

In addition to managing your own output, you will often need the effort and output of other people to do good work in modern organizations. That is to say, you will often need to ask for and rely upon the favors of others in order to do "good work."

Imagine that you oversee a cross-functional initiative, such as leading product development or running a communication initiative. You will undoubtedly need to leverage resources from elsewhere in the organization. You will need other people—people who do not report to you—to give their own time and effort to help you do *your good work*.

Sometimes intangible things make it possible for you to do good work. Perhaps you need a favor to keep a project moving or to secure a signature on a purchase order. Other times you may need help from an ally to influence a decision or shape the direction of a product. Favors abound in atmospheres of good will and trust, the hallmark of a good internal network.

And of course, all of this is a two-way street. In a healthy organization, people will come to you with their own requests for favors and information. Your allies will count on you to use your influence where you can to further their cause. In all but the most isolated professions, good work is only possible when supported by a web of mutually beneficial relationships—brought to life by the constant exchange of favors and information. That is to say, good work is only possible in an environment where everyone is actively and effectively networking.

Right Work

While doing good work is necessary for a successful career, it is far from sufficient. Good work is minimum table stakes. In addition to producing quality results, you must also be working on the right stuff: projects and initiatives that are relevant, valuable, and in line with the strategic direction of the organization. To do that, you need to know who's who and what's what.

You need to be connected. Markets shift. Organizations evolve. You need to know who and what is important in the organization, both today and down the road. Using your networking skills to understand what people are working on, their drivers, and their constraints will impact what you do now and shape what you do in the future. This helps to ensure that you are working on the right things — the things the organization needs and values both today and tomorrow.

Earlier in my career, I learned the hard way to pay attention to what was going on in the larger organization, to ensure that I was working on the right stuff. I had led several initiatives in the IT infrastructure department of a large Silicon Valley company and had developed a reputation as a project wrangler. At first my boss would parachute me into troubled projects, and I would help get them back on track. Soon I introduced the concept of program management when it became clear that several related efforts would be better managed as unified programs rather than as disparate projects.

Then, one day I sat down to see just how many projects and initiatives were competing for time and precious resources in our organization. I compiled a spreadsheet with every project currently active within IT infrastructure. The results were astounding. In an organization of about 600 people and fewer than 450 individual contributors, we had 520 active projects! There was no way that 450 people could simultaneously work on 520 projects. We were desperately in need of a project management office (PMO), a unified list of projects (a portfolio), and a systematic approach to prioritizing and staffing projects (project portfolio management). I campaigned for just such an initiative and not only got the green light but also received a generous budget to hire consultants to lend their expertise. So far, so good.

Then we locked ourselves in a conference room, complete with walls of whiteboards and an endless supply of Post-It notes, and set to work on developing an approach to enterprise project and portfolio management that would best serve our little corner of the world. We emerged six months later, proud as punch, with our new Portfolio Management Plan. It was a comprehensive approach to optimizing the resources across the entire IT infrastructure organization. It was good work.

Unfortunately, it was not the right work. We were dismayed to discover that, during our self-imposed seclusion, we had become completely irrelevant. In the six months that we had been sequestered in a conference room, a competing initiative had emerged on the software side of the house and was being rolled out across all of IT. The CIO supported their initiative. Our initiative never saw the light of day.

By not being better plugged in to the broader organization, we not only wasted six months of time and money, but we also missed the opportunity to provide our input to the design and configuration of the tools and processes that we would ultimately be required to use.

Lesson learned. Figuring out the right and relevant work for the organization requires being well connected, enabling you to do the right work.

Be Visible

Finally, to be successful—and especially to advance—in a modern career, you must be visible. You must see and be seen. You must know who the influencers are and they must know you. At the very least, they must know *of* you. You want to be top of mind when people think of work that needs to be done that you can do.

Consider the film industry's prowess in both production and marketing. What does it take to make a Hollywood blockbuster? To be sure, you have to make a good movie. A Hollywood hit requires a great script, a gifted cast, a masterful director, music, sound, crew, editing… you get the idea.

But a good movie will languish in obscurity if no one knows about it. In addition to incorporating a great product, a successful movie also requires effective, and often extensive, marketing. It's not uncommon for the marketing and promotional expenditures of a movie to be at least as large as, if not many multiples of, the production budget. For example, a movie that cost $100 million to produce may have

accrues to those who can influence decisions, call in favors, and drive change.

Power is a funny thing. Many people are afraid of it, possibly because more than a few people abuse it. The truth is that whenever two or more people are gathered together, there is a power dynamic. Parents have power over their children, teachers over their students, and bosses over their employees. In organizations, power is an omnipresent invisible force woven through the organization that begs to be understood, harnessed, and leveraged. Most important, power is not something to shy away from; power just is.[79]

Some people are troubled by the idea of power. We are often socialized as children to suppress our personal power. "Don't get too big for your britches," as my mom used to say. As a result, many of us grew up with the misguided notion that power is bad or to be avoided. If you find yourself of this mindset—uncomfortable with the thought of acquiring or using power—try substituting the notion of "influence," instead. Seek not to be powerful but to be influential. In healthy organizations, power and influence are essentially synonymous.

Sources of Power

Identifying where the power lies in an organization can be an elusive task at first. It is tempting to just look at the org chart and assume that rank and title confer power. We might call this hierarchical power. Sure, a senior vice president will likely have more power than an individual contributor will have. But if that individual contributor is also the best friend of the CEO's daughter, the power dynamic might not be so clear. Seasoned insiders will tell you that there is minimal correlation between the organizational chart and the actual flows of power in an organization. Power is much more subtle, and significantly more nuanced, than merely rank and title suggest.

Where do you look to see the effects of power in your organization? How do you trace the tendrils of influence? It can be difficult to see the sources and flows of power in an organization directly. However, if you know what to look for, you can see its effects. It's as if you don a pair of "power" glasses and see the organization from an entirely new dimension. It is not unlike looking at a night scene with a thermal imaging[80] camera.

While academics undoubtedly have countless ways to identify power in organizations, it is sufficient for our purposes to understand that power primarily manifests in the ability to make decisions. For example, to say that "someone has power over you" is to say that said person can make decisions that affect your life or well-being. When looking at complex organizational systems, the evidence of power is in plain sight: look for where and how decisions are made, and there you will find the sources and flows of power. For what is leadership but an endless stream of decisions? Big decisions. Small decisions. Go? No-go? Hire? Fire? Go to market? Or head in a different direction?

How People Make Decisions

To understand how decisions are made is to understand power and influence in an organization. Once we understand *how* decisions are made, we can focus on *influencing* those decisions. That is, we can focus on influencing the *people* who make those decisions. It will come as no surprise, therefore, that influencing decisions is where our networking skills — as well as our network — will come into play.

I have long been a devout student of the decision-making process. It is fascinating to observe how people move from uncertainty to certainty in countless situations in their lives. Observing myself and others over a long period of time, I discovered two fundamental characteristics of decision-making, which I have distilled into two simple traits. They seem almost self-evident now. Understanding the machinations of how they work will allow us to apply our networking skills to navigate complex organizational systems with grace and aplomb.

Trait 1: No one makes a decision in an instant.

We often think of decisions as a punctuated moment in time. The moment before the decision, our world was one way, and the moment after, our world is different. Except decisions don't happen that way.

No one makes a decision in an instant. We ease our way into decisions, especially big ones. Decisions take time to incubate and take shape. Our thinking evolves as the viability of various choices ebbs and flows. Eventually we reach that distinct moment when one of the available choices becomes dominant, we flip the switch, and the decision is made. However, the decision didn't just happen. Much has transpired in the background to get us to that "decisive" moment.

Marketing and sales people understand this part of the decision-making process all too well. They warm us up to the idea first and then nudge us along in our thinking, gently but steadily, until we reach that magical point when we make the decision to part with our hard-earned money. Think about the classic techniques that a car dealership will use to try and influence your decision to buy a new car:

- First, they will get you to just come into the showroom, usually through relentless ads and promotions.
- Once they get you into the showroom, and without much obvious pressure, they will invite you to "just sit in the car to see how it feels."
- At some point you will be encouraged to take it for a test drive.
- Then you will go home and think about it (it's rare that you would buy the car on the first visit).
- Some dealerships encourage you to take the car home overnight or even for the weekend.
- Finally, you will decide that you are ready to buy.

All this influencing happens over an extended period—days, weeks, even months.

Trait 2: No one makes a decision in a vacuum

Second, and central to our efforts in networking, decisions are made against a backdrop of other people. No one makes a decision in a vacuum. We often think of decision-makers as isolated oracles of wisdom. They are frequently characterized as lone wolves. "It's lonely at the top," as they say. "I am the decider," George W. Bush proclaimed. We imagine walking into their office, presenting a compelling argument, and standing in awe as the decision-maker decrees a decision before our very eyes. Nothing could be further from reality. With all due respect to George W. Bush, that's just not how decisions work, at least not good ones.

We are social creatures, surrounded by people we respect and trust and who, we hope, feel the same way about us. Because of that mutual respect, the people around us have influence over us. We all live at the epicenter of our very own sphere of influence — the orbits around us filled with people whose input we seek, whose opinions we value, and whose respect matters to us. We are also corporate creatures, with a web of stakeholders to whom we are responsible and accountable.

As we inch our way toward decisions, we look to these stakeholders and trusted advisors for information, validation, input, and feedback. Think back to the example of buying a car. Not only would you not make such a decision in an instant, but you would seek input from many sources that you trust. In organizations, these individual spheres of influence intersect and interact to form networks of influence. Therefore, to get decision-makers to reach a decision, you must also convince all the key people who influence and respect these decision-makers. In fact, you would be wise to influence the influencers long before you present the decision-maker with the call for a decision.

This is where your internal network comes in. Not only can you influence specific decisions at all levels in the company, but you will also be able to shape the direction of entire teams and organizations. A well-networked individual is a powerful force who can disperse ideas and leverage influence throughout their network. Not only might this lead to decisions in your favor, but the quality of decisions throughout the organization will improve in lockstep with the quality and extent of internal networking.

The Influence Map

Sometimes using your network to influence change or specific decisions requires a more formal approach. An *influence map* is a natural extension of the classic discipline of stakeholder management practiced in most project- and change-management methodologies. It goes beyond merely understanding and systematically communicating with your stakeholders, and actively manages the influence among them.

Step 1: Define Your Objective

Start with a clearly defined objective. What are you trying to accomplish? Influence maps are built on individual objectives, not people. In fact, you will likely have multiple influence maps and they will look significantly different, even with all of the same people involved. Examples may include:

- A project you are driving;
- A significant organizational change initiative;
- Getting promoted;
- Getting hired;
- Your career.

Step 2: Identify the Players

Next, identify the people who are relevant to your objective. A person is relevant to your objective if they have the power or wherewithal to positively or negatively influence your objective. These people will fall roughly into one of three categories.

- *Allies or advocates:* people who agree with your objective. These people support and help you achieve what you are trying to accomplish.
- *Adversaries:* people who are adversarial to your objective. Defining someone as an adversary has nothing to do with whether they are a good or bad person. They often have competing drivers or misaligned incentives that make

them at odds with what you are trying to accomplish. For the purposes of an influence map, we care only if they are adversarial to your initiative, your project, your position, or your career.

- *Neutrals:* people who are indifferent to you or your initiative. They have the means to impact your objective positively or negatively but have no particular reason or incentive to do so.

Step 3: Map the Influence

Write the names of all the players on a sheet of paper or a whiteboard, spaced out with room to draw circles and arrows around the names. Using colored pens, choose a color for each category of player—allies, adversaries, and neutrals—and draw a colored circle around each name.

For example, you might use a green pen to circle the advocates, yellow for neutrals, and red for adversaries. Let the diameter of the circle reflect the level of influence each person has over your objective: the larger the potential impact, the larger the circle.

Now step back and study the diagram taking shape. Draw arrows between players that reflect who influences whom. You are looking for ways that you can use your allies to minimize the impact of the adversaries. Ideally, you would convert adversaries to allies, or at least neutrals. If you can't convert them, then look for ways to isolate their impact.

Add more influencers. For every direct player on your influence map, there are countless people in their orbit who influence them in positive ways. These range from bosses and direct reports to high-performing employees and administrative assistants. Add these names to the orbits of your allies and adversaries. Look closely. There is a lot of influence flowing through an organization. Your goal is to begin to identify how that influence ebbs and flows and how you might amplify the positive influence to achieve your objective.

Step 4: Influence

Using your influence map, leverage relationships with your allies to endear the neutrals to your objective, and aim to convert, neutralize, or isolate your adversaries. Language, messaging, and communications are essential to influencing change. Work your network. Ideas flow through an organization in much the same way that a drop of ink diffuses through a glass of water.* Some of the greatest moments of my career in large organizations have been when I intentionally seeded ideas at various points in my network, only to have them make their way back to me days, weeks, or months later.

Example: The Anatomy of a Promotion

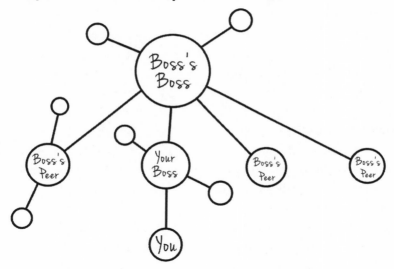

Let's use the example of being promoted to demonstrate the rules of decision-making and an influence map in action.

Promotions are mysterious things. Why do people so often toil in obscurity, passed over for promotions and career opportunities despite excellent work? Why do others — often mediocre performers at

---

* There are numerous mesmerizing videos on YouTube of this diffusion phenomenon. This one is particularly good: "Ink Drops 4K (Ultra HD)," *YouTube*, January 30, 2013, youtu.be/k_okcNVZqql.

best — receive the plum opportunities and rise through the ranks? It's easy to fall into the misconception that to get promoted, all you need to do is deliver good work — or inversely, that because you have done good work, you will be promoted. In his excellent book *Power: Why Some People Have It — and Others Don't*, Stanford University Professor Jeffrey Pfeffer pulls back the curtain on the relationship between job performance and promotions:

> The data shows that performance doesn't matter
> that much for what happens to most people
> in most organizations. That includes the effect
> of your accomplishments on those ubiquitous
> performance evaluations and even on your
> job tenure and promotion prospects.[81]

So how, then, does one manage to get promoted in the modern organization? The first step is to shift your focus from your boss to your boss's boss. As much as you feel beholden to your immediate manager for any advancement in your career, the reality is that your direct boss has limited power to get you promoted. The decision on whether to promote you will generally be made at the next-highest level in the organization, by your boss's boss.

For the sake of our influence map, let's draw your boss's boss in the center of the page with a large circle around them. This person has the most power to grant your objective.

The next step is to embrace the fact that no one makes a decision in a vacuum. The salary action to promote you will depend not just on the strong recommendation of your boss but also upon the endorsement *of everyone else who reports to your boss's boss*. Let me say that again: to get a promotion, you will need to have convinced — or at least be in excellent standing with — everyone who reports to your boss's boss. Each of your boss's peers, sitting around the table in a staff meeting, will need to think of you as ready and worthy of a promotion. This is no small task.

And since none of these key people (your boss and his or her peers) makes a decision in a vacuum, you have to acknowledge that they each have allies and adversaries. Before long, your influence map will be full of circles and arrows with the many players and their influencers.

Finally, embrace the fact that no one makes a decision in an instant. You may need to spend months strategically working the influence map before your promotion occurs. Be visible to these people. Make sure that your network—and especially the ultimate decision-makers—are fully aware of your aspirations for higher-level work.

To be promoted it is necessary for most of the people on your "Get Promoted" influence map to be able to visualize you in the new role.* Focus on tasks and deliverables that help them in that visualization. Ask for more responsibility and then deliver on it. Even better, use your understanding of what the organization needs—achieved through your deep networking—and sculpt a new role that maximizes the value that you can provide to the organization.

Then, over time, work the influencers on your influence map to seed and water the idea of the need for such a role. Inch them toward the realization, and the ultimate decision, to promote you into the role. The reality is that no one makes a decision in an instant, and no one makes a decision in a vacuum. Using your internal network to embrace these realities equips you with tremendous power and influence in any organization.

Exercise: Influence a Promotion

If you are currently employed, create an influence map for your next promotion. Remember that your boss's boss will make the ultimate decision on your promotion.

Key

- The size of each circle reflects the amount of influence a person has on a decision to offer you a promotion.

---

* This is true for hiring as well. To get a job offer, the hiring manager, along with most of the interview team, must be able to imagine you in the role. Steer your performance during the interview process to facilitate that visualization.

- The color of the arrows indicates whether the influence is positive, neutral, or negative:
  - Green: Advocate
  - Black: Neutral
  - Red: Adversary

Identify the Players

1. Start with a circle for your boss's boss at the center of the map.
2. Add circles for the people who influence your boss's boss, including your boss and all of your boss's peers.
3. Since your boss will be the primary advocate for your promotion, add circles for the people not already on the map who influence your boss.
4. Using appropriate colors for advocate, neutral, and adversary, draw arrows between the circles that reflect the flows of influence.

Strategy

The influence map visually addresses the reality that nobody makes a decision in a vacuum. Your strategy also needs to account for the fact that no one makes a decision in an instant.

- Develop a general strategy to influence people over time as to your worthiness of a promotion. Do not talk specifically about wanting a promotion in the early stages of executing your strategy.
- Strengthen your reputation among all players on the map. Look for ways to take on high-profile projects and be more visible.
- Develop strategies to win over your neutrals and win over, or neutralize the influence of, your adversaries.
- With all the groundwork in place, let your advocates know that you are seeking a promotion.

Chapter 27

Networking At Work: The Players

It's not what you know, but who you know.

Old Adage

We are now ready to get down to specifics regarding the ins and outs of building an internal network. I've talked a lot about why you want to build a robust network in your organization. Let's get into the "how" of it all. Here we will extend our networking mindset and expand our external networking tools so that you can use them inside complex organizations.

Setting out to build a network in your organization can feel overwhelming at first, particularly for people who are shy or have a preference for introversion. What makes this approach so effective — and what hesitant people may find comforting — is that it takes a systematic approach to building a network by using consistent language and an agenda structured to enhance collaboration and cohesion in the organization. Everyone can be successful with this approach.

Further, networking efforts in an organization have a multiplier effect.[82] Like our original networking principles, this approach to inside networking reaches beyond individuals to leverage the inherent interconnectedness of organizations. Not only will your ideas spread through the organization, but your efforts will be amplified. Good behaviors are emulated. Good relationships are contagious.

In writing the next two chapters, I ran into a bit of a chicken-and-egg problem. Networking in an organization is a little more involved than networking with the general population. While an extension of the basic networking principles, inside networking is more deliberate in its outreach and more substantial in its exchange of information.

The problem was what to present first: the people you reach out to or the topics you talk about? If I present the key players first, it will be hard to imagine what you would talk about with some of these people. If I start with the talking points, you will have a hard time imagining to whom you would address such questions.

In the end I decided to start by looking strategically at the key players you'll want in your network. In the next chapter, we'll delve into specific talking points on what we should discuss and share in our networking conversations. I recommend that after you finish the next chapter, reread this one with the talking points in mind.

Key Players

The first step to building a powerful internal network is to think strategically about who should be in it. All of us have a network over-weighted with connections that came through serendipitous encounters and unprompted introductions. But again, a career—and now a company—is far too important to leave to chance, good fortune, and happy accidents. Build your internal network deliberately. Develop a plan and look for key players anywhere in your organization. Do not be constrained in your planning by rank, title, or location. Networking is non-hierarchical. There are no limits to the people you can include in your network.

However, while there are no limits, there are certainly some risks, especially if you get over-zealous in your internal networking. Organizations have natural immune systems. You will trigger that immune system's defenses, and antibodies will start swarming around you if you start by knocking on the doors of the most senior executives in your company or reach out to people who seem too far afield from your daily responsibilities.

The best way to build a network in your organization is to work systematically in ever-widening circles, starting with and reaching through people who are logically related to your work. Not only will you build a stronger network, but you will also build alliances and trust along the way. Further, by systematically expanding your reach, your intentions and good reputation will precede you. To get you started, here is a minimal set of recommended internal network connections.

Teammates

Start nearby. As a collaborative team member, you must thoroughly understand what everyone on your team brings to the table, what they are working on, how they work, and how their work contributes to the success of your (shared) boss. Start by getting to know every one of the people who report to the same boss that you do. While this may be obvious, I have met too many people who only had the vaguest sense of who they worked with and what those people did. If you are in a new role—and especially if you are newly hired—conduct introductory meetings with each of your teammates within the first month of your arrival on the team.*

Peers

Beyond your immediate team, start to network horizontally across your company. The key here is to look for peers with whom you interact on a regular basis and with whom you have roughly the same level of responsibilities. Is there a manager, director, or project manager with whom you interact regularly? Weave them into your network. Are you a member of any special committees or task forces? These people are your peers. All are potential people to add to your network.

Stakeholders

The term "stakeholders" has emerged into our corporate language in the last several decades, concurrent with the rise of large, complex organizations and the evolution of project management. Stakeholders are

---

* See my Individual Jump-Start for help in mapping out what you need to learn, who you need to meet, and what you need to accomplish when you step into a new role. heatherhollick.com/helpful-individual-jump-start.

people with shared interests, people impacted by your work, or anyone who may have an impact on your work. Whatever your responsibilities, whether they relate to a project, a product, a team, or a function, the efforts and outcomes of your work will affect people. These people are your stakeholders. The larger the potential impact, the more important the stakeholder. Feel free to reach out and network with all these people.

Conversely, anyone whose roles and responsibilities can have an impact on you or your work is also a stakeholder. The impact could be either positive or negative. In fact, one of the quickest ways to identify stakeholders is to ask yourself, "Who, if they were so inclined, could wreak havoc for me?" These, too, are your stakeholders and are good candidates for people who can be woven into your network.

Finally, don't limit your networking vision to internal stakeholders. There will be vendors and external partners who fit the definition of "stakeholder" as well, especially those who can impact *your* work (see the sidebar on vendor management in the next section). Try to network and build relationships with them as well.

Leaders of Support Organizations

After you have established a solid base of teammates, peers, and key stakeholders, expand your network into cross-functional support organizations. Included in this category are departments such as human resources, finance, IT, sales, marketing, and so forth. Leaders in these organizations have a tremendous ability to impact your work and your long-term success.

Further, I have found that the people who gravitate to such fields are often driven by a desire to be helpful and supportive. Understanding what these groups are working on, along with their drivers and constraints,[*] can make for powerful network allies.

---

[*] We will delve more deeply into drivers and constraints in the next section.

Your Boss's Peers

Regardless of what your job description says, your primary responsibilities are to help your team be successful and make your boss look good. To that end, some of the most important people you want in your internal network are your boss's peers—the people who report to the same person your boss reports to.

Think about this for a moment. Your boss—let's call her Sue—will, along with several peers, report to someone higher in the organization—let's call him Mike. Mike will have a broad area of responsibility for which he is accountable and that he will have distributed among his various direct reports—Sue and her peers. Mike will also have his own drivers and constraints that he will communicate to these direct reports.

Further, organizations take on the personality of their leaders. Mike will have his own style, personality, and interpretation of the company culture, which will manifest in the culture of the various teams that report to him. Understanding all that is happening across all his teams will provide tremendous insights into how your organization works, what is important, what you should work on, how to deliver your best work, and how to make your boss look good.

Be forewarned, however, that the cadre of your boss's peers is also the group with whom you must tread the most carefully. Your boss can easily feel threatened if you proceed to have one-on-one conversations with his or her peers, without complete transparency and before you have built sufficient trust.

Warm your boss to the idea over time. Explain that you would like to conduct informational interviews with each of their peers, and be clear on your intentions. Share the questions you intend to ask. Engage them in your mission of learning and spreading goodwill by asking if they would pave the way for your conversations by letting their peers know that you will be contacting them. Most important, report back what you observe and learn.

Lest you think that building relationships with your boss's peers is optional, remember that no one makes a decision in a vacuum. If you

231

have any responsibilities that have any impact beyond your own team, you will want to be visible to these leaders. And, as we discussed above, if you ever expect to get a raise or a promotion within your current chain of command, you will have to not only convince your boss to go to bat for you, but you will also need to be in good standing with an overwhelming majority of your boss's peers (see "Anatomy of a Promotion" in Chapter 26). Your boss and your boss's peers are some of the most important potential allies in your entire inside network.

Your Boss's Boss

If you're with me so far, then your network and your career will be in great shape. If all you did was build your internal network based on all the players we have already mentioned — peers, stakeholders, leaders of support organizations, and your boss's peers — you would be very well connected. You would also be tapped into significant information networks, have your finger on the pulse of organizational priorities, and wield a significant amount of organizational power.

But wait, there's more. If the culture of your company permits, you might want to look higher and farther for additional people to include in your networking strategy. First on that "higher and farther" list is your boss's boss.

Before you start sending out calendar invitations to your senior VP, carefully assess the culture of your company regarding employees going around their boss and requesting to meet with leaders higher up the organization. In other words, is it okay to request a skip-level meeting? A skip-level meeting is corporate jargon for any meeting in which a leader meets with one or more employees more than one level down the chain of command. For example, a VP meets with a manager, skipping the director that sits between them in the org chart.

Skip-level meetings are standard practice in many companies, whereby senior leaders reach down a few levels into the organization for informational meetings, one-on-ones, and coffee klatches. In such companies, these meetings are part of the culture, endorsed and encouraged at all levels. Good skip-level meetings not only provide valuable, bidirectional communication up and down the ranks, but they also stimulate employee engagement and allow younger leaders to gain visibility into higher-level priorities and decision-making. In such cultures, it would be perfectly natural to request a networking meeting with your boss's boss.

Not all company cultures, however, are so enlightened. We're talking about a *reverse skip-level meeting:* one in which the lower-level employee reaches up two or more levels of the hierarchy to initiate a meeting. Trust your instincts and proceed with caution. Prepare your boss, making it clear that your intention is to build mutually beneficial relationships, foster collaboration, and enhance your ability to perform in your current role. If you do it right, meeting with more-senior leaders in the company can be deeply rewarding and beneficial for all participants. Also, visibility. Did I mention visibility?

Other Movers and Shakers

As mentioned in the chapter on mentors and mentoring, building relationships with movers and shakers in your company can be a powerful addition to your network. Who are the bright lights and the rising stars in your company? Who is leading the key projects? Who has visibility beyond where you can see now? All of these people are great candidates for your network.

Approach senior leaders in the company with an air of gratitude and respect. You may benefit from working with a mentor before you are ready to meet some of these movers and shakers. As we discussed, a mentor can not only tell you who you should know, but they can also help you prepare to meet them. If you are lucky, they can make a warm introduction for you as well. This is how the best networking works, and it is particularly powerful when you practice it inside your organization.

This is a good time to point out that not all networking meetings need to happen on company time. Meeting people outside of work—especially over coffee, lunch, or happy hour—is a great way to connect while neutralizing some of the hierarchy inherent in most company cultures.

At this point you are probably asking yourself, "How could I possibly reach out for a networking meeting with some of these people? What would I say?" Fear not. Your intentions are pure. With the right questions and a willingness to exchange favors and information, you can meet with just about anyone in your company. Let's get to the talking points.

Chapter 28

Networking At Work: The Talking Points

If you could get all the people in an organization rowing in the same direction, you could dominate any industry, in any market, against any competition, at any time.

Patrick Lencioni[83]

Now that we know which people we want in our internal network, let's cover what we'll talk about with these people, especially during our initial conversation. Like any potential network connection, these efforts initiate from similar motivations: looking to be helpful and building a mutually beneficial professional relationship. However, in a work environment their connection runs much deeper and their impact is much broader. We inherit a bond with colleagues based on our shared commitment to the same company. As a result, the nature and structure of these internal conversations require a technique that is tailored to an audience of fellow employees.

Here are the basic questions for networking conversations with colleagues:

1. What are you working on?
2. What are you priorities?
3. What are your drivers?
4. What are your constraints?

Let's explore each one.

Q1. What Are You Working On?

As with all networking encounters, the very best opening volley is the quintessential networking question, "What are you working on?" In a work environment, however, rather than the delightful ambiguity of the question—which often leads to curious, interesting, and sometimes deep conversations—coworkers will naturally assume you are asking what they are working on for the company. This is a good thing. Knowing what other people are working on helps you put your work in context and will suggest possibilities for ways you can be helpful. This is the essence of a collaborative mindset, made possible by a simple five-word question.

If the person with whom you are meeting is socially skilled, they will reciprocate with the same question. Even if they don't ask directly or use the same wording, I implore you to share what you are working on. Collaborative cultures require that everyone has at least a general sense of what other people are working on.

Besides, this is, after all, a networking conversation. People want to be helpful. Make it as easy as possible for them. You never want to go into an internal networking meeting without being prepared to talk about what you are working on. As you prepare, think about the resources they have available to them, who they know, and what they know. Then frame what you are working on in a way that they find easy to understand. Make it easy for them to find a way to tap into their own desire to be helpful. If you already know a way in which they might be helpful to you, don't hesitate to ask for a favor.

Don't worry if you do not mutually exchange favors during your first meeting. I would estimate that something sharable comes to mind in the moment less than 10 percent of the time. It's the desire and the intent that count. You might think of something that might be helpful tomorrow, next week, or next month. It's the spirit of helpfulness and the mindset of collaboration that will have the biggest impact in the long term.

Q2. What Are Your Priorities?

The next bullet in your talking-points memo is priorities. Understanding other people's priorities allows you to see new dimensions of the organization. Priorities determine where people choose to focus their energy and how they allocate their time. They also vary from person to person and team to team. Most important, priorities are linked to your time horizon. For example, you will have very different priorities for a week, a quarter, a year, and the rest of your life. It's as if you are zooming in and out of different time frames. For networking conversations at work, the best level of priorities to explore with colleagues is the range of the next three months. A three-month horizon will give you the best perspective for understanding how you might be helpful.

Most of the time, I can infer a person's immediate priorities based on what they talk about, especially when they share what they are working on. However, discerning their priorities for the next three months might be less obvious. Don't be afraid to ask. I have always found that people appreciate the opportunity to clarify their priorities, both to themselves and to their colleagues.

Note also that everyone has both official and unofficial priorities. When building relationships with people, it is helpful to pick up on both. Your colleague may have an official priority to get a project done by the end of the month and an unofficial priority of clearing her in-box before she leaves for vacation at the end of the week. Both provide valuable insights into how the organization works and opportunities for you to collaborate and be helpful.

Q3. What Are Your Drivers?

The third bullet in your talking-points memo is drivers. The area of drivers opens the door to some of the most profound and important conversations you can have with colleagues. While priorities are the goals we set to *pull ourselves forward*, drivers are the intrinsic and extrinsic forces that *propel us*. Drivers tell us much about organizations and the people who work in them. They are nuanced and diverse. Drivers can range from broad organizational principles outlined in corporate objectives to subconscious personal motivations of which people might not even be aware.

To unpack the power of understanding drivers, I have deconstructed them along two dimensions: organizational vs. personal and explicit vs. implicit. This gives us four unique combinations to explore. Note, however, that in a general conversation I would never ask more than, "What are your drivers?" The multidimensional details are for my own understanding. Besides, the explicit drivers, especially the organizational ones, are easy to discover. And the implicit drivers, by their very nature, are below the surface and not openly expressed.

Explicit Drivers — Organizational

Explicit drivers are relatively easy to spot. At their most basic, they are the things upon which people are measured. Senior leaders, for example, are often driven by metrics such as their contribution to revenue or market growth. Consider these examples as well:

- Human resource leaders might be measured by the quality of the leadership pipeline.

- Recruiters might be driven by the number of candidates in the hiring pipeline or the number of positions filled.

- Digital marketing people might be measured by website hits or the level of activity on social media.

- During my days in IT infrastructure, managing data centers full of humming servers, system availability and server uptime were the drivers for my team and me.

- I once ran an IT help desk. The number of open support tickets was one of the primary drivers of my team.

Explicit organizational drivers are often manifestations of codified organizational expectations. For example, everyone has corporate and team objectives. These objectives are typically rolled out at the beginning of a fiscal year and cascaded down through the company. These objectives become drivers. Further, objectives are often translated into formulas for annual bonus calculations. How people are paid affects their behavior. Ask someone how their annual bonus will be calculated. Their answer will reveal one or more of their explicit organizational drivers.

Explicit Drivers — Personal

Individuals have explicit *personal* drivers, in addition to team and organizational drivers. Perhaps you are managing a large project, complete with a detailed plan flush with tasks and dates. Nestled within the project milestones and deliverables will be a rich source of personal drivers. If you are a product manager at any level or part of a software development team, then release dates and other deadlines define your life. These are drivers.

Everyone who has ever worked in a large organization is familiar with some form of the individual performance development plan (IDP) or personal development plan (PDP) and the annual performance review. Nestled somewhere in every IDP is a handful of performance "objectives" against which you will be evaluated during your annual performance review.* These explicit, personal performance objectives become personal drivers. I am not saying that I would ask someone to share their confidential personal development plan with me. Rather, people have external factors that manifest as drivers that, in turn, influence their behavior. Understanding their drivers (as well as your own) helps teams work and enables people to collaborate much more effectively.

If you want to quickly tap into someone's explicit personal drivers during a networking conversation, simply ask them some variation on the question, "How are you measured?" Alternatively, you might ask, "How do you know if you are doing a good job?" or "How will your bonus be calculated?" The answers to these questions point directly to some of their explicit drivers.

---

* I dream of the day when annual performance reviews are a distant memory. Recent trends are encouraging, including companies such as Microsoft and Eli Lilly, which are moving away from a single annual review toward more frequent, low-pressure conversations about performance and expectations. See Chana R. Schoenberger, "How Performance Reviews Can Harm Mental Health," *The Wall Street Journal*, October 26, 2015. bit.ly/helpful_performance.

Implicit Drivers — Organizational

By their very nature, implicit drivers are more difficult to discern than explicit ones. Implicit drivers are implied and not openly expressed. Don't let their elusiveness deter you. Even though they aren't written down anywhere or aren't part of any bonus calculation, rest assured that their presence is ubiquitous and inescapable. Most important, given their subconscious existence, it turns out that they are also much more powerful than explicit drivers, significantly influencing individual behaviors and the direction of the organization. Once you learn what to look for, you will see them at work everywhere.

Implicit drivers at the organizational level are often found in the cultural norms and unwritten rules that shape expectations and influence behaviors. If you've ever heard someone say, "Let me explain how we do things around here…" you've found yourself about to be schooled in a cultural norm. Over time these norms coalesce into powerful forces that drive behaviors across the organization.

One place that implicit organizational drivers tend to manifest is in the decision-making process. Pay close attention to the requirements, processes, levels of authority—even the rituals—that lead to decisions. Therein you will find some of the organization's most important implicit drivers.

When I worked at the tech giant Cisco Systems in Silicon Valley in the early 2000s, frugality was a prominent cultural norm. We had all heard the legend of how the CFO would cut off the long sleeves of his dress shirts to make them into short-sleeved dress shirts appropriate for summer.* We got the message. The expectation of frugality influenced every project proposal, every line-item in every budget, and every hiring decision. While we were not measured in any formal way on frugality, it was a significant factor in any decision and a powerful driver in the organization. By continually reinforcing frugality as a cultural norm, Cisco had succeeded in making frugality an implicit organizational driver.

---

* In hindsight this sounds absurd to me now. But we heard the story often, sometimes from the CFO himself, and we took it to heart.

At the same time, Cisco's motto was, "Changing the way we live, work, play, and learn." We all believed it. We cited it as our mantra. We bragged about "drinking the Cisco Kool-Aid." Without being told to do so directly, we made innovation an implicit driver of everything we did.

The Implicit Driving Power of Culture

Countless implicit drivers lurk just below the surface in most organizations. Take a closer look at the organization's culture and you will discover a broad array of powerful, implicit drivers. "What is culture?" you ask. If I search for that phrase via Google I get more than 1.7 billion results. One of the top results is

> ...culture is defined as the shared patterns of
> behaviors and interactions, cognitive constructs,
> and affective understanding that are learned
> through a process of socialization.[84]

While that may be an academically rigorous definition of culture, it is not very helpful in our exploration of team cultures. Over the years, the more I studied organizational behavior, the more I wanted a definition of culture that would clarify the culture of the organization while also providing a framework that would allow me to influence change within the organization.*

I came to the realization that you can think of an organization's culture quite simply as the personality of the group. Describing people's personalities is easy. As adults we develop a natural ability to intuit the characteristics and qualities that form an individual's distinctive character.

In the same way that individuals have personalities, groups develop personalities as well.† Groups have a voice of their own, a mind of their

---

* This is not unlike what we did when we were seeking to define a network. We settled on a definition that allowed us to derive a robust model of networking.

† I posit that whenever two or more people come together, they create a "meta-being," a collective mind that has a personality, a will, even a voice of its own. Alas, that is a discussion appropriate for a more philosophical text.

own, a will, even their own metabolism. Think about the mind and will of a group that is marching in Washington, D.C., or the metabolism of a city like New York.

The personality of a group applies to collections as small as two — a relationship — all the way up to entire populations of cities and countries. Miami has a personality, as does Hong Kong. The United States has a personality, as does the United Kingdom. The personalities of Miami and Hong Kong are markedly different, as are the personalities of the US and the UK.

Similarly, each company has a personality. And each team within a company has its own unique personality, usually reflecting the leader along with some variation on the personality of the entire company.

Defining culture as the personality of the group clarifies an elusive concept. The idea of personality is something we seem to understand intrinsically. If I ask you to describe the personality of your best friend, you will have no trouble defining the characteristics and traits that define that person. And so, by calling culture "the personality of a group," we have a sense of what that means. We also have various concepts and tools that help us understand the personality of individuals. I have yet to find one of these individual concepts that did not also help me understand the organizations in which we live and work (see sidebar for Personality Assessment Tools).

Unfortunately, the concept of personality can be a bit nebulous as well. Lest we get too far afield into the subtleties and nuances of culture, let's remember that our mission in this section is to find ways to uncover implicit organizational drivers. With that in mind, the very best framing of culture (and personality) that I have discovered is simply the *attitudes, behaviors*, and *beliefs* of the organization. These familiar concepts are easy to wrap our heads around and give us something to work with when attempting to understand a culture.

What are some of the prevailing attitudes in your organization? What are the dominant behaviors? What are some of the core beliefs that people ascribe to when they decide to work there?

Here are a few of my favorite examples that incorporate attitudes, behaviors, and beliefs to describe the culture of large organizations.

- Think about the culture of the large financial firms on Wall Street. Wall Street firms are well known for confident, even brazen, *attitudes* and aggressive *behaviors*. These characteristics define their culture and point directly to some of their drivers.

- What do we know about the cultures of Google and Facebook? Both internet giants *believe* strongly in the power of data—big data. This belief drives not only the actions of individuals within the companies but also contributes greatly to the direction of each company.

- What about Apple? Apple reveres iconoclasts,* which manifests in an *attitude* of marching to their own drum. Apple also believes that individual privacy is of utmost importance. As a result, privacy and respect for others are powerful drivers throughout the company.

- In more general terms, Silicon Valley companies often make big bets on the future, while insurance companies, by their very nature, are more risk-averse. Each of these cultures embrace different *attitudes* and *beliefs* about risk and the future, which, in turn, lead to different drivers within their organization.

One other place to look when trying to discern an organization's personality is the most senior leaders in the company. Organizations take on the personality of their leaders. How would you describe the personalities of the most senior executives in your company? Further, how do they work together? If you can articulate the personality of the senior leadership *team*, you can likely describe many characteristics of the personality of teams at all levels in the organization.

---

* As part of their 1997 "Think Different" campaign, Apple ran an ad called "Here's to The Crazy Ones," which showed their reverence for iconoclasts. See "Apple – Think Different – Full Version," *YouTube*, youtu.be/cFEarBzelBs. Accessed February 7, 2019.

Personality Assessments

Individual personality assessments have been around for a long time. I have found that various assessments developed for individuals can also generally adapt and apply to the personality of an organization.

For example, as a Myers-Briggs practitioner, I love to assess an organization along this instrument's dimensions (introversion/extraversion; sensing/intuition; thinking/feeling; judging/perceiving). It quickly becomes plain that, just as individuals have preferences for introversion or extraversion, organizations do as well. My experience living in the UK taught me that, as a culture the United Kingdom has a marked preference for introversion, which is in sharp contrast to my experience in the US, where the personality of the culture leans toward extraversion. Like most large groups, the population of America and of the United Kingdom have roughly the same split between individual preferences for introversion and extraversion. And yet, at the collective level of the countries, the overall culture of each displays a noticeable preference for one over the other.

Implicit Drivers — Personal

In addition to inheriting all the implicit drivers of an organization, each individual brings a panoply of their own motivations, incentives, and stimuli to the party. While we could spend a lifetime exploring the nooks and crannies of individual personalities to ascertain implicit personal drivers, we're not going to do that here. Entire fields of academic research, matched by rich genres of self-help and personal-psychology literature,* are dedicated to the subject. The purpose here is simply to raise awareness of their existence so that you can figure out how you might be helpful to a colleague.

Unfortunately, no one is going to come right out and describe their implicit drivers. They are, after all, implicit. However, with a little

---

* A particularly relevant book in this category is *Drive: The Surprising Truth About What Motivates Us* by Daniel Pink. Speaking primarily to knowledge workers, Pink deconstructs intrinsic personal motivation into three basic components: desire for autonomy, desire for a sense of purpose, and a need for mastery.

curiosity and a dash of empathy you can learn much about a person. I have found it useful to ponder some of the following questions when I am trying to understand someone's implicit drivers:

- What motivates this person? Why do they get up in the morning? Why do they stay at this company? In this position?

- How ambitious are they? How anxious are they to make progress?

- Where are they in the arc of their career? Are they just getting started or close to retirement?

- What are their personal priorities?

- What are some of their beliefs? What do they believe about work and about themselves?

- What are some of their core values?

- How would you describe their default attitude toward their work, their colleagues, and the company?

- How strong is their need for recognition? Do they thrive on being in the spotlight, or do they shine in their own quiet way?

- How strong is their need for affiliation? Some people just want to get along. For these people, it is often essential that the workplace have a warm and friendly atmosphere. They value working with interesting people and would not think about rocking the boat.

- How competitive are they? How much do they value getting ahead, being promoted, winning, and making more money?

- How strong is their desire for personal growth? To some degree everyone has a desire for personal growth and mastery of their craft—after all, to be alive is to be growing. However, this desire varies widely. Some people thrive on personal challenges and proving themselves.

Any organization—even those with the strongest, most well-defined, most homogeneous cultures—will be home to a broad mix of individual personalities, each moved to action by a wide variety of implicit drivers. Once you start to identify the various drivers of members across your organization, you begin to see things from an entirely new perspective. I liken it to donning a pair of x-ray glasses. Suddenly you see energy and intention that you didn't know existed. What was once a blur of humanity becomes a mosaic of individuals colored by their preferences and drivers.

Grid Of Drivers

	Explicit	Implicit
Organizational	How are you measured? Corporate and team objectives Team and company bonus factors Corporate mission statements	Cultural norms "How things are done" How decisions are made
Personal	Personal performance objectives Bonus factors Milestones Deadlines	Motivations Ambitions Beliefs Values

To bring this all back together, learning about other people's drivers helps us to build relationships more effectively. And mutually beneficial relationships are the heart of networking and collaboration.

Career Insider's Tip #1: Never get in the way of someone's drivers.

If you would like a long and prosperous career, whatever you do, never get in the way of someone's drivers. Instead, do what you can to *augment* people's drivers, and encourage their success in the *direction of* their drivers.

While this should be obvious, I have encountered many people in my life — myself included — who were bowled over by ambitious people whose drivers put them at odds with what I was trying to accomplish. If you want to enjoy your job, never get in the way of the implicit and explicit forces that move someone.

Q4. What Are Your Constraints?

The fourth and final area in our core inside-networking conversation topics is constraints. While drivers are the forces that propel us, constraints are those things that hold us back. Everyone has constraints, as does every team and every company. We all encounter headwinds from time to time.

People tend to be more forthcoming about their constraints than they might be about their drivers. I usually come right out and ask, "What are your constraints? What is holding you back?" Some constraints will be explicit headwinds and impediments. Money is often a constraint, a limited budget or tight funding. People constraints are common — having the right people and having enough of them can often be a challenge. Time is the eternal constraint — is there ever enough time? The ability to grow and scale can be constraints.

Every company has both *explicit* and *implicit* organizational and cultural constraints, just as they have both types of drivers. One company where I worked had an inordinately powerful legal department. It seemed that everything we did — and I truly mean darn-near everything — had to be approved by someone in the legal department before we could proceed. Constantly looping in the legal department was a constraint.

Often the reporting structure of an organization can introduce implicit constraints, as can corporate policies and procedures. Take a close look at the organizational chart and I bet you will find bottlenecks and constraints scattered throughout.

And, of course, every individual has *implicit* personal constraints as well. We all have circumstances, habits, and beliefs that hold us back. We may have a fear of failure, lack confidence, find ourselves averse to confrontation, or simply be missing the gene that helps us stay organized. We may be too cautious, too passive, or too risk-averse. All these internal battles can manifest as personal constraints. When we learn to recognize constraints in others, we can quickly adapt to working more effectively with them, even helping to shore up their weaknesses.

Career Insider's Tip #2: Never add to anyone's constraints.

If you would like a long and prosperous career, never amplify, augment, or contribute to anyone's constraints. Instead, in the spirit of being a collaborative employee and a master networker, do whatever you can to minimize their constraints, regardless of the source.

So What?

What do all these interpersonal and psychological insights have to do with networking and collaboration? To begin to understand another person's drivers is to begin to understand how they see the world, how they act, and how they are likely to act. Their drivers shape where they channel their energy and how they make decisions. Given that a mutual spirit of helpfulness is essential to innovation and collaboration, if you want to find ways to be helpful to someone, you will be most effective if you look in the direction of their drivers.

Similarly, understanding other people's constraints will help you gain deeper understanding of their limitations, perceived and otherwise. Your insights into what makes them tick and what holds them back will make you a more effective collaborator. You will have realistic expectations of what they can accomplish and a much better sense of how you might be helpful.

Don't Be A Doormat

In addition to always being on the lookout for ways to be helpful, remember that you are not a doormat. Every healthy networking relationship is mutually beneficial. It's collaborative. Assume that other people's intentions are as well-meaning as yours are. That is, assume that, like you, people want to be helpful.

By assuming good intentions, we unleash powerful forces in inter-personal relationships. At the very least, we allow for the positive inter-pretation of potentially ambiguous words or actions. More important, we project our high expectations that other people are acting with good interests beyond just their own. People have a way of living up to our expectations.

Do your best to help people help you. Think about their world and their domain of expertise. It is unlikely that you would talk to your mechanic about a medical prescription or your doctor about an oil change, even though you may need both. Conversations and requests are always contextual. Use your heightened awareness of other people's drivers to shape the context of your interactions. When you're sharing what you're working on — and especially when you are looking for help from someone else — let *their* drivers and *their* constraints shape and guide *your* requests.

Rethinking Office Politics

Office politics are notorious for wreaking havoc on many a career. I believe, however, that office politics in most organizations are widely misunderstood. Often maligning office politics as an endless web of power plays and self-aggrandizement, many people perceive their work environments to be somewhere between *House of Cards* and *Mad Max*. While there is no shortage of dysfunctional organizations powered by inept leaders who enable counterproductive behaviors, labeling the culture "political" is less than helpful. Too many people in these envi-ronments opt to keep their head down and stay out of the fray.

The worst thing you can do is to try and stay out of the fray alto-gether. You ignore what is perceived as office politics at your own peril. You can't just avert your eyes and hold your breath, wishing for a bet-ter work environment. Deeply human emotions and ambitions power the dynamics that manifest as political behavior. These emotions and ambitions can be harnessed and leveraged when they are acknowledged and understood. The good news is that by simply reframing how you think about politics and office dynamics, you can both thrive in a "political" environment and become a powerful influencer who can work wonders in bringing alignment across the organization.

Misaligned Drivers

What if all the perceived political players aren't playing politics at all? What if it is much simpler than that? What if most dysfunctional organizations are merely a result of misaligned drivers and unmanaged constraints? Of course there are plenty of bad leaders out there, but consider this a useful working hypothesis.

Imagine, for example, that you could draw a graph of vectors representing just the explicit organizational drivers of all the mid-to-senior leaders in an organization. A vector is a two-dimensional quantity from mathematics and physics that indicates both magnitude *and* direction. A political vector would show the strength of political power, indicated by the length of the line and the direction in which the power was pulling.

Our political vectors would show arrows of all different sizes pointing every which way. The marketing team is pulling in one direction, the IT group, with much less force, might be pulling in another. The sales teams are screaming for new customers, while the support teams are struggling to take care of existing customers. Before long, the graph of your drivers starts to look like a pile of pick-up sticks.

And these are just the organizational drivers. Now imagine layering in the personal drivers of some of the leaders involved. Imagine a director who is dead-set on making VP by his fortieth birthday, and you have more conflict and tension than the tug-of-war at a bikers' rally.

Framing political behavior in terms of drivers and constraints changes the landscape. Don't think of it as political at all. Assume that people have good intentions and that internal politics come about not because most people are malicious, self-serving, and don't like each other but because they have competing or conflicting drivers and, to a lesser degree, unmanaged constraints.

It's not always that simple. There are definitely a few malicious and self-serving people in all levels of leadership positions who create office politics for their own purposes. But not everyone is self-serving. Most people are well-intentioned, just biased towards their drivers and blind to their constraints. By assuming good intentions, acknowledging others' drivers, and minimizing constraints wherever you find them, you can have a tremendous positive influence on any organization.

If you set out to discover others' drivers and constraints, you will gain valuable insights that will help you build your internal network and work more effectively. And the knock-on effect will be that you raise people's awareness of often-undiscussed issues and set in motion a cascade of beneficial conversations that will lead to less politics, more productive outcomes, and more positive change.

Organizational Alignment

Most people have an innate sense that everyone in an organization should be pulling in the same general direction. And yet, when people think of an organization being aligned, they assume that this emanates from the executive suite. Indeed, most executives see that organizational alignment is their responsibility. But what do they mean by alignment? My experience is that most senior leaders have a concept of alignment that is too abstract to be of much practical value to the organization.

A February 2017 article in *The Harvard Business Review* sheds light on how senior leaders should be thinking about organizational alignment. In "How Aligned Is Your Organization?"[85] two business-school professors describe the enterprise-alignment process in terms of these building blocks: enterprise purpose, business strategy, organizational capability, resource architecture, and management systems. Uh, ok. Define a purpose, set a course, ensure capabilities exist, provide resources, and provide systems that make it possible to get work done. These are all key elements of a functioning business.

But organizational alignment goes much deeper than merely aligning corporate strategy with resource architecture (whatever that is). Alignment is a deeply human, interpersonal state of collaboration and coworking. It involves heightened levels of awareness and a mindset biased toward collaboration and coworking. As noted at the beginning of this chapter, Patrick Lencioni, in his brilliant "leadership parable" says, "If you could get all the people in an organization rowing in the same direction, you could dominate any industry, in any market, against any competition, at any time." Think about that for a moment. Are all the people in your organization rowing in the same direction? It is reasonable to ask if all the people in the organization are even rowing at all, let alone in the same direction. Indeed, many people appear to be rowing, but their oars aren't touching the water. And a small but significant portion of the organization may actually be drilling holes in the boat.

But what if you *could* get all the people in an organization rowing in the same direction? How does an executive create that kind of alignment at the interpersonal level? What is the "organizational capability" that leads to everyone rowing in the same direction?

This is where the inside-networking conversation comes in. The ongoing, open discussion of drivers and constraints among a broad cross-section of colleagues and peers is one of the most powerful and important conversations that organizational members can have. Over my thirty years of working, observing, and influencing in organizations, I have become convinced that 99 percent of all political and dysfunctional behavior results from misaligned drivers and poorly understood constraints. Aligning them is possible only when a critical subset of the employee population commits to expressing, discovering, and understanding the invisible web of drivers and constraints.

To thrive in the modern organization, bring the ideas of drivers and constraints to the surface broadly and frequently. Integrate what you discover with the way you work and interact with others. By leading the charge in these networking conversations, you will not only thrive in most work environments, but you will also be a catalyst for greater efficiency and enhanced collaboration. You will be driving alignment at its source — the interpersonal interactions between people and teams.

Two Bonus Networking Questions

To be a networking powerhouse in your organization, all you need is to equip yourself with the first four questions in this chapter for your inside-networking conversations: What are you working on? What are your priorities? What are your drivers? And what are your constraints? As relationships mature, however, it's helpful to get deeper insights into the person you are working with, to forge a more meaningful relationship. For that, I offer two additional questions that I often ask when networking with people inside of an organization.

Q5. Who Are Your Best People?

One of the quickest ways to get insights into a person's values and leadership style is to ask them to tell you about a couple of their best people. Listen for clues about why they consider them to be so valuable. While the person (typically) waxes poetic about one of their star players, they will also be speaking volumes about their own values and preferences. This is valuable information when you are trying to build mutually beneficial relationships.

As a further bonus, the people they mention will be great candidates for connections in your network. They see them as movers and shakers and the go-to people for getting things done. Think back to the influence map we discussed in Chapter 26. These people are influential. The top performers identified will have considerable ability to influence this leader. These people are valuable to note and to know.

Q6. Who Else Should I Talk To?

If you connect on a human level with people you meet, then ideas and people will begin to flow through their mind as they are talking. Their brain is making connections for you. You are wise to leverage their active mental processes as best you can. Further, the people they recommend will also provide valuable insights into how you are perceived.

If they suggest that I talk to someone senior or powerful, I sometimes ask, "What do I need to know or do to be ready to meet them?" This question works on multiple levels. It honors the breadth of their network and shows that you respect their reputation with that person. It opens the door for them to think of additional people beyond the ones that immediately came to mind. Finally, it shows that you are willing to learn, and invites them to see potential in you.

Vendors, Suppliers, and Contractors

Modern organizations leverage a wide variety of contractors, freelancers, vendors, and suppliers. Each of these resources will have a single point of contact within the company who is tasked with managing the relationship. Some people think that the art of vendor management is to squeeze every vendor for as much as you can from every transaction. This is nothing more than the ideology of a playground bully.

I recommend a different approach. Managing suppliers and vendors is just a variation on the theme of inside networking. Interactions with vendors are also mutually beneficial relationships in a wide web of professional relationships. You want your vendors to be profitable—not too profitable, mind you, but profitable. You need them to see value in this relationship and want them to continue to work with you for the long haul. You want them to provide their best products, assign their best people to the account, and deliver top-notch service. To do all that, they have to be profitable and see your relationship as mutually beneficial.

Enter the networking conversation. Strive to build an ongoing, networking relationship. The framework fits perfectly. When you know what they are working on, you can look for ways to be helpful—perhaps by introducing them to a potential client or referring someone from your network who would be ideal for their organization. When you both develop a mutual understanding of each other's drivers and constraints, you can each shape your expectations in ways that amplify your respective drivers and minimize your constraints. You will be amazed at the tremendous service, output, and loyalty you get from your vendors.

General Recommendations

By now you can see that the inside-networking conversation is a bit more focused and nuanced than general, professional networking. Now that we know who we are going to talk to and what we're going to talk about, here are a few final guidelines for building a powerful network in your company.

- Regardless of how long you have been in your role or at your company, it's never too late to start building a network.

- Your best bet is to start early and build systematically. As I mentioned in Chapter 27 in the section "Key Players," I recommend a specific approach of expanding your network in concentric circles.

- Leverage your first ninety days in a new role. Building a network is particularly important, effective, and powerful during your first few months in a new position. When you start a new role, and especially when you start with a new company, you have a honeymoon period of about ninety days to get your bearings and start building relationships. People will not think twice if you reach out and ask for thirty minutes of their time. When you request meetings with people, frame it as you trying to get your bearings and learn as much as you can. No one will even bat an eye at your request.*

- Keep your intentions pure. Your goal is to improve your effectiveness and find ways to be helpful. Radiate these intentions. By understanding what is going on in other parts of the organization, you hope that you can be more collaborative. And by gaining insights into other people's drivers and constraints, you expect to enhance the value you and your team will be able to provide.

- Be transparent. Sometimes bosses can get nervous if you are meeting with their peers, their boss, or anyone beyond their span of control. If your intentions are pure, you (and the boss) should have nothing to worry about.

- Be fully cognizant that as you build a network, you are amassing influence and power. Use it wisely and strategically.

- Alignment is everyone's responsibility. Understanding drivers and constraints is how you do it at the grassroots level.

- The time will come when you need to ask for help or a favor. When it does, you will have a better sense of who to ask, what to ask for, and how to ask for it. Note that if you are not periodically asking for favors, then you are not leveraging your network to its fullest potential. You are probably not collaborating all that much, either.

- If you remember nothing else from this book, remember that the secret to success is to augment people's drivers and minimize their constraints. Never do the opposite.

If you do all these things, you will be doing good work, you will find yourself drawn to the right work, and you will be visible. These are the fundamental elements of career success.

---

* See my Individual Jump-Start for a concise approach to planning for your first three months in a new role. It can download at **heatherhollick.com/individual-jump-start**.

Talking Points Summary

Now that you have the framework of drivers and constraints, reread Chapter 27. Imagine asking these questions to each of the key players:

1. What are you working on?
2. What are your priorities, especially for the next three months?
3. What are your drivers?
4. What are your constraints?
5. Who are your best people?
6. Who else can I talk to?

Exercise: Organizational Drivers

Review a broad range of factors that influence behaviors in your organization. Read through the corporate mission and vision statements. Watch or listen to speeches and public presentations from your most senior executives. Develop a list of the resulting explicit and implicit drivers.

Explicit Drivers

- How are you measured?
- What are your corporate objectives?
- What are your team objectives?
- What are your team and company bonus factors?

Implicit Drivers

- What attitudes, behaviors and beliefs are espoused?
- What are some of your cultural norms — "how things are done around here"?
- How are major decisions made?
- How do the personalities of the CEO and the executive leadership team influence behavior across the organization?

- How does the personality of your boss influence behavior across your team?

Exercise: Personal Drivers and Constraints

Use this exercise in two ways. First, use it on yourself as an introspective exploration of yourself, your role, and your understanding of the company. Then, use it regularly as a template for conversations that you have with colleagues across the company.*

1. What Are You Working on?

- *At work:* What are your team and corporate goals, objectives, projects, deliverables, and so forth?
- *In your career:* What are your professional- and leadership-development goals and ambitions?
- *In life:* What are your personal goals and ambitions?

2. What are your drivers?

- What are the *explicit* organizational goals, objectives, and metrics that motivate and propel you?
- What are the *implicit* organizational and cultural expectations that shape your behaviors and performance?
- What motivates and drives you *personally?*

3. What are your constraints?

- What are the *explicit* impediments and headwinds that slow you down?
- What are the *implicit* organizational and cultural constraints that impede your progress?
- What are the *personal* circumstances or beliefs that inhibit your growth?

---

* All of the exercises in this book are included in *The Workbook of Helpful Exercises* and can be downloaded at heatherhollick.com/helpful.

Chapter 29

Informational Interviews Within Organizations

Results are obtained by exploiting opportunities, not by solving problems.

Peter F. Drucker

As discussed in general in Chapter 21, informational interviews are a great way to deepen your understanding of a company, expand your visibility in your organization, explore new career directions, find a mentor, and even fashion new opportunities. They are particularly potent when used as part of an inside-networking strategy. As you seek to deliberately build your internal network, informational interviews can often open doors.

Be deliberate and strategic in your requests for informational interviews. Colleagues and coworkers are busy. You can't just request a chunk of someone's time without a darn good reason. People want to know why you want to meet with them and how they might prepare. We have already established two broad categories of opportunity to build and nurture relationships with colleagues:*

1. You are still in the honeymoon period of a new role and are using the opportunity to get to know as many people as possible;

---

* Although a regular strategy of meeting colleagues for lunch is an excellent networking strategy that doesn't require much justification beyond the tried and true, "We should do lunch sometime."

2. You are connecting with stakeholders who are impacted by the work you do or the responsibilities you bear.

But what if you want to meet with someone else in the company? What if your honeymoon period is over and the person with whom you would like to meet does not fit the definition of a stakeholder? Enter the informational interview. When all else fails, the premise of an informational interview as the purpose of a meeting opens the entire company to your network.

There are a host of reasons that you might want to meet with someone. To name just a few:

- You truly admire them as a leader and would like to learn from them.
- You are looking for collaborative opportunities across normal organizational boundaries.
- You are looking for ways to enhance the value that you can provide to the company.
- You are looking for a mentor.
- You are looking for other career opportunities within the company.

As with any informational interview, the general guidelines apply:

- Leverage your network. You will have the most success if you proceed by way of a warm introduction from someone you already know.
- Honor people's time. Request twenty-five or fifty minutes; then stick to it.* If the conversation runs beyond the requested time, avoid the temptation to keep talking. Ask if it would be better to schedule a follow-up conversation.
- Be clear on your reasons for requesting the interview.
- Be prepared with an arsenal of good questions. You won't get to all of them, but that's okay.

---

* Twenty-five- or fifty-minute meeting requests are better than thirty- or sixty-minute requests because they reinforce your respect for people's time. Everyone appreciates having a five-to-ten-minute buffer between meetings.

- Do your homework. Be prepared with a good understanding of the experience, background, and responsibilities of the person with whom you meet. Don't ask questions that you could have found the answers to elsewhere in the company. Use company websites, LinkedIn, or any other information in advance as part of your homework.
- Don't talk too much. Be prepared to answer questions, but your principal role is to ask them.
- Use your full arsenal of networking questions, including, if appropriate, the inside-network conversations about priorities, drivers, and constraints.
- Finally, as always, be a good networker. Find out what they are working on, and look for ways to be helpful in return.

Chapter 30

Final Thoughts

Almost everything that happens in life is the result of a network. Making, or breaking, local links is the way to change.

Deborah M Gordon[86]

I used to be afraid of networking. I allowed my preference for introversion and my general lack of social skills to distort my understanding of how careers work. I allowed fear to keep me from putting myself out there, based on a couple of unfortunate experiences that distorted my understanding of networking. I was afraid of being rejected. Now I understand that networking is about being helpful. It's about leveraging who you know and what you know to help other people be successful—and surrounding yourself with other people who do the same.

People can't reject me anymore. It's not that I learned to protect myself; it's that I no longer put *myself* out there to be rejected. Instead, I extend an offer of goodwill. I engage with a spirit of helpfulness. If they reject my offer to be helpful, to tap into my knowledge, my experience, and my network, well, I'm happy to find that out as soon as possible and move on. They may have rejected my help, but they haven't rejected me.

Networking has become essential to our personal and professional lives. It is how we do good work and how we know what is the right work to do. Networking is also essential within our modern organizations. Internal networks are the nervous system that makes collaboration and alignment possible.

Most people bumble through building and maintaining a network without giving it much thought. Can you imagine what will happen when a significant number of us start embracing the world with this spirit of helpfulness and this approach to networking? Can you picture the brightness and thickness of the interconnected links and the vastness of the interconnected networks? I can.

When I was young I mindlessly subscribed to the Judeo-Christian belief that we are here to dominate the Earth. This egocentric—some might even say narcissistic—belief never sat well with me. Domination seemed self-serving and shortsighted. As I grew older I began to see that we are not above nature at all. Like many of you, I began to see that we are part of nature.

Writing this book at a time when our political and cultural norms appear to be collapsing has awoken in me the profound realization of how deeply interconnected we are. And not just as humans. We are deeply interconnected as living organisms as well. A flood of recent research shows that our microbiome—both *on* and *in* our bodies—is made of cells that belong to other organisms.[87]

This deep interconnectedness goes beyond just our biological, organic systems. From global economics to the behavior of ants, better minds than mine are beginning to understand the complex interactions of our global systems. International trade is no longer simple or bilateral. Our communities, towns, states, and countries are deeply interdependent.

We are not just part of nature. We *are* nature. It's your career and it's your life. But it's our world. I urge you to make the most of it.

Be helpful.

Be collaborative.

Be visible.

Be powerful.

Be connected.

And for the sake of us all, go forth and network.

Before you Go

My purpose in writing this book was to help foment a grass-roots revolution in the way we support one another, especially as it relates to the ways in which we earn our livelihoods. Now that you have made it this far, you are part of that revolution. Welcome to the worldwide tribe of people who are embracing the world with a spirit of helpfulness.

I would love to hear from you. How have these ideas changed the way you live, work, play, and learn? Are you networking differently? Are you building better relationships? Better teams? Better companies?

Feel free to drop me a line at hello@heatherhollick.com. You will also find a cornucopia of additional ideas and information on my website at heatherhollick.com.

I look forward to your email,

Heather
February 2019.

Acknowledgments

Where to begin? This book wasn't so much written as it was assembled from the aspirations and insights of the countless people whose lives have intersected mine over the years. I am eternally grateful to the friends, leaders, and thinkers who shared my journey in one way or another.

I thank the Haas Alumni Network, and especially Tenny Frost, for that first opportunity to pull my thoughts together, at Homecoming in 2007, on how our alumni network could become more powerful. I remain indebted to the ongoing support from my Haas Alumni Network and the support of the global chapters.

Out of that one presentation, a movement was born. I am grateful to the dozens of event organizers over the years who took a chance on an unknown speaker who thought she had something to say. Their events and the feedback from the participants have helped to shape and hone the ideas in this book. An extra tip of the hat to La Tondra Murray for giving me so many opportunities to share and grow with the students in the Masters of Engineering Management Program at Duke University. And, most of all, I thank the thousands of audience members who attended my talks on networking and careers over the years. Their attentiveness, questions, feedback, and, in many cases, our ongoing relationship have enriched this content and my life in innumerable ways. I hope I have been a good steward of their passions.

I am humbled to have learned from so many leaders at the top of their game. I have been forever changed by Stephen White, the best boss I ever had, for his acknowledgment of my potential and his keen insights on organizational communication and the influence map. I was blessed to work under the leadership of Kenny Robertson during my time in the UK. His strong preference for extraversion was matched only by *my* equally strong preference for introversion. Yet, he showed how the two forces are complementary and how we could work together in a powerful combination that leveraged our respective strengths. And I thank my friend Robert Williams, a master networker who approaches a crowd with grace and refined elegance. He is a model of how to network for those of the extravert persuasion.

I am in awe of the intellectual giants upon whose shoulders I stand. I am indebted to Keith Ferrazzi for his magnificent work in *Never Eat Alone*. I am inspired by Mark Horstman and Michael Auzenne, of "Manager Tools," for their pioneering work in podcasting and their brilliant work in the areas of management, interviewing, leadership, and careers. I am emboldened by Nick Corcodilos, of "Ask The Headhunter," for his fearless thought leadership on searching for a job and getting hired. And I will be forever grateful to Bob Allard and Richard Banfield for their brilliant manifesto, *The Care and Feeding of Your Network*. It was they who introduced me to the powerful networking question, "What are you working on?"

It takes a village to nurture a book into existence, and I am deeply grateful to the bevy of people who have lent me their time and talents to make this one real. I feel as though I won the lottery when I connected with Ashleigh Imus as my editor. She understood what I was trying to accomplish. Buoyed by a gentle spirit, her depth of knowledge has made every page better. I am grateful to have found her and hope we will see many more projects together.

Thank you to the generous souls who read early versions of this book and offered insights and feedback. Shout-out to Brad Irby, Jessica Clayton, and Caitlin Lorenc for taking the time to make extensive notes and comments. I am humbled and grateful for their insights and suggestions.

I owe much to the example and encouragement of Jeff Smith, friend, family, and role model. I am grateful for his ongoing assurances and for showing me how it's done through the writing and publication of his own book, *Becoming Amish.*

And finally, my deepest gratitude goes to my spouse and partner, Linda Gottschalk, whose support and career enabled a lifestyle for us that made my coaching and writing possible. Her insights into corporate life are sprinkled throughout the pages of this book. Further, our life together has taken us on a nomadic journey that forced me out of my shell. I suspect that my networking skills would have remained dormant if not for her confidence and comfort in social situations. I'm hoping that the adventure is just beginning.

About the Author

Heather Hollick is a speaker, writer, facilitator, and coach on a mission to make the world a better place to work. She is an expert in helping people navigate complex organizations and build satisfying careers. She is also adept at helping leaders create strong teams and vibrant organizations.

Heather has an MBA from the University of California at Berkeley, a master's degree in applied mathematics from Purdue University, and an undergraduate degree in math, physics, and secondary education.

Speaking and coaching are Heather's third career. After almost a decade as a high-school and college math and physics teacher, she made the leap to the corporate world, where she developed into a seasoned IT leader, managing data centers and large projects for such diverse entities as Cisco Systems and the Pensions Department of the British Government.

Not only is Heather on her third career, but she has earned her networking stripes through total immersion. She recently moved for the twenty-ninth time since heading off to college. Born in Canada, she has lived and worked in seventeen cities and towns, eight US states, three countries, and on two continents. In each new place she hit the ground running, starting with little more than her existing network, a clear networking strategy, and a dogged determination to connect with people.

Endnotes

1. Epictetus, *The Art of Living*, A New Interpretation by Sharon Lebell, (New York: HarperOne, 2013), Kindle Version, p. 42. Epictetus was an ancient Greek Stoic philosopher. There are no known original writings of Epictetus but his lectures were compiled by one of his students in two works: *The Discourses* and *The Enchiridion*. In T*he Art of Living*, Sharon Lebell offers a selection of the ideas from these two works. Her goal was to communicate the authentic spirit, but not necessarily the letter, of Epictetus using language that would give fresh expression to what she thought that Epictetus would have said today.

2. Circa 2004-2005.

3. George Monbiot, *Out of the Wreckage: A New Politics for an Age of Crisis* (London: Verso Books, 2017), Kindle Locations 152–53.

4. "Mirror Neuron," *Wikipedia,* https://en.wikipedia.org/wiki/Mirror_neuron. Accessed February 4, 2019.

5. Joseph Henrich, *The Secret of Our Success: How Culture Is Driving Human Evolution, Domesticating Our Species, and Making Us Smarter* (Princeton: Princeton University Press, 2016).

6. Monbiot, *Out of the Wreckage*, Kindle Locations 205–15.

7. See, for example, Karen Cheng's accounting of her year-long quest to become a good dancer: "Girl Learns to Dance in a Year

(TIME LAPSE)," *YouTube,* https://youtu.be/daC2EPUh22w. Accessed February 4, 2019.

8. See "I Yam What I Yam," *Wikipedia,* https://en.wikipedia.org/ wiki/I_Yam_What_I_Yam. For a video clip, see the incorrectly named post "I ams what I am," *YouTube,* https://youtu.be/wae1j-aCD1o. Accessed January 31, 2019.

9. For more on the curious city in the desert, and the fascinating story of the London Bridge, see "Lake Havasu City, Arizona," *Wikipedia,* https://en.wikipedia.org/wiki/Lake_Havasu_City,_ Arizona. Accessed February 4, 2019.

10. See "California Gold Rush," *Wikipedia,* https://en.wikipedia.org/ wiki/California_Gold_Rush. Accessed February 4, 2019.

11. See "Dot-com bubble," *Wikipedia,* https://en.wikipedia.org/ wiki/Dot-com_bubble. Accessed February 4, 2019.

12. This quote is often attributed to Oscar Wilde, although I found no substantive evidence that he made this remark.

13. "Extrovert or extravert?" *The Grammarphobia Blog,* January 11, 2016, https://www.grammarphobia.com/blog/2016/01/ extrovert-extravert.html. Accessed February 4, 2019.

14. See Susan Cain, *Quiet: The Power of Introverts in a World That Can't Stop Talking* (New York: Random House, 2012). See also Sophia Dembling, *The Introvert's Way: Living a Quiet Life in a Noisy World* (New York: Penguin Group, 2012) and Jennifer Kahnweiler, *Quiet Influence: The Introvert's Guide to Making a Difference* (San Francisco: Berrett-Kohler Publishers, 2013).

15. Susan Cain, "The Power of Introverts," *TED,* February 2012, https://www.ted.com/talks/susan_cain_the_power_of_introverts. Accessed February 4, 2019.

16. For an excellent exposition of the differences between shyness and introversion, see Susan Cain, "Are You Shy, Introverted, Both, or Neither (and Why Does It Matter)?" *Quiet Revolution,* http://www.quietrev.com/

are-you-shy-introverted-both-or-neither-and-why-does-it-matter. Accessed February 4, 2019. See also David Robson, "Why We Should Celebrate Shyness," *BBC Future,* August 31, 2016, http://www.bbc.com/future/story/20160830-why-we-should-celebrate-shyness. Accessed February 4, 2019.

17. Cain, *Quiet,* p. 10.

18. Cortisol is a hormone released by the adrenal gland in response to stress.

19. See, for example, Lindsey Kaufman, "Google got it wrong. The open-office trend is destroying the workplace," *The Washington Post,* December 30, 2014, http://wapo.st/1Bjk6EE. Accessed February 4, 2019.

20. Anne Frank, *The Diary of a Young Girl* (New York: Anchor Books, 2001), p. 207.

21. A full Meyers-Briggs assessment with a certified MBTI practitioner can be an enlightening experience.

22. Martin Jones, *Twitter,* July 25, 2014, http://bit.ly/2sGjjUg. Accessed February 4, 2019.

23. For more insight into employee referral programs, see "Employee referral," *Wikipedia,* https://en.wikipedia.org/wiki/Employee_referral. Accessed February 4, 2019.

24. Daniel J. Boorstin, *The Discoverers* (New York: Random House, 1983), Kindle Edition, p. 86.

25. Henry Melvill, "Partaking in Other Men's Sins," sermon, *The Golden Lectures* (London: James Paul, 1855), p. 102.

26. Keith Ferrazzi and Tahl Raz, *Never Eat Alone, Expanded and Updated: And Other Secrets to Success, One Relationship at a Time* (New York: The Crown Publishing Group, 2014), Kindle Edition, p. 188.

27. Edgar A. Guest, *The Path to Home* (Chicago: The Reilly & Lee Company, 1919), p. 43.

28. Ferrazzi and Raz, *Never Eat Alone,* Kindle edition, p. 81.

29. "Keepalive," *Wikipedia,* https://en.wikipedia.org/wiki/Keepalive. Accessed February 4, 2019.

30. Ferrazzi and Raz, *Never Eat Alone*, Kindle edition, p. 198.

31. Richard Bach, *Illusions: The Adventures of a Reluctant Messiah* (New York: Random House Publishing Group, 1977), Kindle Edition, locations 581–92.

32. Ferrazzi and Tahl, *Never Eat Alone,* p. 188.

33. Steve Dalton, "Harness the Ben Franklin Effect, Boost Your Career," *The Huffington Post,* January 17, 2014, https://www.huffingtonpost.com/steve-dalton/harness-the-ben-franklin-effect_b_4605447.html. Accessed April 25, 2018.

34. "Handshaking," *Wikipedia,* https://en.wikipedia.org/wiki/Handshaking. Accessed February 4, 2019.

35. Tip of the hat to Bob Allard's brilliant manifesto on *Change This* called "The Care and Feeding of Your Network." This short pamphlet on nurturing your network first introduced me to the powerful question, "What are you working on?" Bob Allard and Richard Banfield, "The Care and Feeding of Your Network," *Change This,* March 9, 2006, http://changethis.com/manifesto/show/21.CareFeedingOfNetwork. Accessed February 4, 2019.

36. See Wikipedia, https://en.wikipedia.org/wiki/Norm_of_reciprocity. Accessed January 18, 2019

37. Monbiot, *Out of the Wreckage,* Kindle Locations 200–05.

38. Kirsten Armstrong, "Starting Points" *Runners World,* August 15, 2013, https://www.runnersworld.com/women/a20793761/starting-points. Accessed February 4, 2019.

39. "About LinkedIn," https://press.linkedin.com/about-linkedin. Accessed March 28, 2018.

40. Fees for job postings and the premiums that recruiters pay for universal access to anyone who is accepting job inquiries were

LinkedIn's primary source of revenue prior to their acquisition by Microsoft, accounting for 60 percent of their net profit in fiscal year 2014. Source: LinkedIn 2014 Annual Report, http:// www.annualreports.com/HostedData/AnnualReportArchive/l/ NYSE_LNKD_2014.PDF. Accessed February 4, 2019.

41. See Seth Godin, "The power of a tiny picture (how to improve your social network brand)," *Seth's Blog,* http://sethgodin. typepad.com/seths_blog/2009/04/the-power-of-a-tiny-picture-how-to-improve-your-social-network-brand.html. Accessed February 4, 2019. Used with permission.

42. As recently as late 2017 the material was posted on LinkedIn's site at https://www.linkedin.com/help/linkedin/answer/90.

43. "Usenet," *Wikipedia,* https://en.wikipedia.org/wiki/Usenet. Accessed February 4, 2019.

44. Shauna C. Bryce, "How to Be A LION on LinkedIn," *Work It Daily,* https://www.workitdaily.com/linkedin-lion. Accessed February 4, 2019.

45. See, for example, Section 8.2 from the March 20, 2015 capture in the *Internet Archive,* https://web.archive.org/ web/20150320230247/https://www.linkedin.com/legal/user-agreement. Accessed February 4, 2019.

46. See https://www.linkedin.com/premium/products for the complete grid of tiers and features. Accessed February 4, 2019.

47. Find the full fifty-minute podcast at https://www.manager-tools.com/2006/04/secrets-of-a-great-handshake. Accessed February 4, 2019.

48. As quoted by Ron Howard, portraying Jim Lovell in the movie *Apollo 13.*

49. See, for example, "Peanuts Teacher," *YouTube,* https://youtu.be/ XrbumvF-Oe4. Accessed February 4, 2019.

50. Friend of the author.

51. http://asktheheadhunter.com.

52. http://www.manager-tools.com/products/interview-series.

53. http://www.humanworkplace.com.

54. There is no better resource here than Nick Corcodilo's series of eBooks called *Fearless Job Hunting.* In particular, see *Book Six: The Interview: Be The Profitable Hire,* http://www. asktheheadhunter.com/store/fjh/books.htm.

55. The web is awash with great information on informational interviews. Here are a few that I recommend: "Informational Interviewing Tutorial: A Key Networking Tool," *Live Career,* https://www.livecareer.com/career/advice/interview/ informational-interviewing. Accessed February 4, 2019 (a thorough tutorial); Marci Alboher, "Mastering the Informational Interview," *New York Times,* January 29, 2008, http://nyti. ms/1QU4Lqs. Accessed February 4, 2019 (excellent suggestions and a great list of sample questions).

56. See Richard Branson, *Losing My Virginity: How I Survived, Had Fun, and Made a Fortune Doing Business My Way* (New York: Crown Business, 2007).

57. See Jack Welch, *Jack: Straight from the Gut* (New York: Hachette Book Group, 2003).

58. See Tony Schwartz and Jim Loehr, *The Power of Full Engagement: Managing Energy, Not Time, Is the Key to High Performance and Personal Renewal* (New York: Simon & Schuster, 2003).

59. See David Allen, *Getting Things Done: The Art of Stress-Free Productivity* (New York: Penguin Group, 2015).

60. See Linda Hill and Kent Lineback, *Being the Boss: The 3 Imperatives for Becoming a Great Leader* (Boston: Harvard Business School Publishing, 2011).

61. For example, see "Dunning-Kruger Effect," *Wikipedia,* https:// en.wikipedia.org/wiki/Dunning–Kruger_effect. Accessed February 4, 2019.

62. For additional compelling arguments on why you might want to work with a coach, see the brilliant article by Tomek Kwiecinski, "18 Reasons to Go to a Coach or Therapist," *Imprific,* January 8, 2016, https://imprific.com/tomkwiecinski/18-reasons-to-go-to-coach-or-therapist. Accessed February 4, 2019.

63. Spoken by Peter Block to me during a workshop titled *Flawless Consulting*.

64. Charles Duhigg, "What Google Learned from Its Quest to Build the Perfect Team," *New York Times,* February 25, 2016, http://nyti.ms/1QXXPIG. Accessed February 4, 2019.

65. "Performance" was measured in terms of EBITA, earnings before interest, taxes, depreciation, and amortization. See IBM, "Working Beyond Borders: Insights from the Global Chief Human Resource Officer Study" (Somers, NY: IBM Global Business Service, September 2010), https://www.ibm.com/downloads/cas/WQVBAZAM. Accessed February 4, 2019.

66. J. Bughin and M. Chui, "The Rise of the Networked Enterprise: Web 2.0 Finds Its Payday," *McKinsey & Company,* December 2010, https://www.mckinsey.com/industries/high-tech/our-insights/the-rise-of-the-networked-enterprise-web-20-finds-its-payday. Accessed February 4, 2019.

67. Margaret Schweer, Dimitris Assimakopoulos, Rob Cross, and Robert J. Thomas, "Building a Well-Networked Organization," *MIT Sloan Management Review* (Winter 2012): 35–36.

68. John P. Kotter, "What Leaders Really Do," *Harvard Business Review,* December 2001, https://hbr.org/2001/12/what-leaders-really-do/ar/1 or http://bit.ly/1PlQQaj. Accessed February 4, 2019.

69. In the wake of the 2008 financial crisis, many analysts and business commentators began to ask if the big banks, with hundreds of thousands of employees, had become "too big to manage." See, for example, Ben W. Heineman, Jr., "Too Big to Manage: JP Morgan and the Mega Banks," *Harvard Business*

Review, October 3, 2013, https://hbr.org/2013/10/too-big-to-manage-jp-morgan-and-the-mega-banks. Accessed February 4, 2019.

70. John P. Kotter, "Hierarch and Network: Two Structures, One Organization," *Harvard Business Review Blogs,* May 23, 2011, https://hbr.org/2011/05/two-structures-one-organizatio or http://bit.ly/1mvrywi. Accessed February 4, 2019.

71. Jeffrey Pfeffer, *Power: Why Some People Have It—and Others Don't* (New York: Harper Collins, 2010), Kindle Locations 3212–16.

72. Pfeffer, *Power,* Kindle locations 3218–21.

73. Of course, this serendipity starts with your draw in "the ovarian lottery," as Warren Buffet calls it. For more about his views of how lucky he was, see Joe Weisenthal, "We Love What Warren Buffett Says About Life, Luck, And Winning The 'Ovarian Lottery,'" *Business Insider,* December 10, 2013. http://read.bi/1Qs3tiB. Accessed February 4, 2019.

74. Tami Forman, "How to Network Without Feeling 'Icky,'" *Forbes,* September 27, 2017, https://www.forbes.com/sites/tamiforman/2017/09/27/how-to-network-without-feeling-icky. Accessed February 4, 2019.

75. Schweer, Assimakopoulos, Cross, and Thomas, "Building a Well-Networked Organization," p. 36–37.

76. "Minions," *Wikipedia,* https://en.wikipedia.org/wiki/Minions_(film). Accessed February 4, 2019.

77. Schweer, Assimakopoulos, Cross, and Thomas, "Building a Well-Networked Organization," p. 37.

78. Marshall Goldsmith, *Mojo: How to Get It, How to Keep It, How to Get It Back If You Lose It* (New York: Hyperion, 2009), Kindle Edition, p. 165.

79. For more on the phenomenon of power in organizations, see Pfeffer, *Power: Why Some People Have It—and Others Don't.*

80. See "Thermography," *Wikipedia,* https://en.wikipedia.org/wiki/ Thermography. Accessed February 4, 2019.

81. Pfeffer, *Power: Why Some People Have It—and Others Don't,* Kindle Locations 347–49.

82. See "Multipliers," *Wikipedia,* https://en.wikipedia.org/wiki/ Multiplier_(economics). Accessed February 4, 2019.

83. Patrick M. Lencioni, *The Five Dysfunctions of a Team: A Leadership Fable* (San Francisco: John Wiley and Sons, 2002), Kindle Locations 78–80.

84. "What is Culture?" *Center for Advanced Research on Language Acquisition, University of Minnesota,* http://carla.umn.edu/ culture/definitions.html. Accessed February 4, 2019.

85. Jonathon Trevor and Barry Varcoe, "How Aligned Is Your Organization?" *Harvard Business Review,* February 2017, https:// hbr.org/2017/02/how-aligned-is-your-organization. Accessed February 4, 2019.

86. Deborah M. Gordon, "Local links run the world," *Aeon,* February 1, 2018, https://aeon.co/essays/the-most-important-connection-in-any-network-is-the-local. Excerpted from her book, *Ant Encounters: Interaction Networks and Colony Behavior* (Princeton: Princeton University Press, 2010).

87. James Gallagher, "More than half your body is not human," *BBC News,* April 10, 2018, http://www.bbc.com/news/ health-43674270. Accessed February 4, 2019.

Bibliography

Alboher, Marci. "Mastering the Informational Interview." *New York Times,* January 29, 2008. http://nyti.ms/1QU4Lqs.

Allard, Bob, and Richard Banfield. "The Care and Feeding of Your Network." *Change This,* March 9, 2006. http://changethis.com/manifesto/show/21.CareFeedingOfNetwork.

Allen, David. *Getting Things Done: The Art of Stress-Free Productivity.* New York: Penguin Group, 2015.

Armstrong, Kirsten. "Starting Points." *Runners World,* August 15, 2013. https://www.runnersworld.com/women/a20793761/starting-points/.

Bach, Richard. *Illusions: The Adventures of a Reluctant Messiah.* New York: Random House Publishing Group, 1977.

Boorstin, Daniel J. *The Discoverers.* New York: Random House, 1983.

Branson, Richard. *Losing My Virginity: How I Survived, Had Fun, and Made a Fortune Doing Business My Way.* New York: Crown Business, 2007.

Bryce, Shauna C. "How To Be A LION on LinkedIn." *Work It Daily.* https://www.workitdaily.com/linkedin-lion/.

Bughin, J., and M. Chui. "The Rise of the Networked Enterprise: Web 2.0 Finds Its Payday." *McKinsey & Company,* December 2010.

Cain, Susan. "Are You Shy, Introverted, Both, or Neither (and Why Does It Matter)?" *Quiet Revolution.* http://www.quietrev.com/ are-you-shy-introverted-both-or-neither-and-why-does-it-matter/.

———. *Quiet: The Power of Introverts in a World That Can't Stop Talking.* New York: Random House, 2012.

Dalton, Steve. "Harness the Ben Franklin Effect, Boost Your Career." *The Huffington Post,* January 17, 2014. https://www. huffingtonpost.com/steve-dalton/harness-the-ben-franklin-effect_b_4605447.html.

Dembling, Sophia. *The Introvert's Way: Living a Quiet Life in a Noisy World.* New York: Penguin Group, 2012.

Duhigg, Charles. "What Google Learned from Its Quest to Build the Perfect Team." *New York Times,* February 25, 2016. http:// nyti.ms/1QXXPIG.

Epictetus. *The Art of Living,* A New Interpretation by Sharon Lebell. New York: HarperOne, 2013.

Ferrazzi, Keith, and Tahl Raz. *Never Eat Alone, Expanded and Updated: And Other Secrets to Success, One Relationship at a Time.* New York: The Crown Publishing Group, 2014.

Forman, Tami. "How to Network Without Feeling 'Icky.'" *Forbes,* September 27, 2017. https://www.forbes.com/sites/ tamiforman/2017/09/27/how-to-network-without-feeling-icky.

Frank, Anne. *The Diary of a Young Girl.* New York: Anchor Books, 2001.

Gallagher, James. "More than half your body is not human," *BBC News,* April 10, 2018. http://www.bbc.com/news/health-43674270.

Goldsmith, Marshall. *Mojo: How to Get It, How to Keep It, How to Get It Back If You Lose It.* New York: Hyperion, 2009. Kindle Edition.

Gordon, Deborah M. *Ant Encounters: Interaction Networks and Colony Behavior.* Princeton: Princeton University Press, 2010.

Grad, Shelby, and David Colker. "Nancy Reagan turned to astrology in White House to protect her husband." *Los Angeles Times,* March 6, 2016. http://lat.ms/2e8wzYk.

Heineman, Ben W., Jr. "Too Big to Manage: JP Morgan and the Mega Banks." *Harvard Business Review,* October 3, 2013. https://hbr.org/2013/10/too-big-to-manage-jp-morgan-and-the-mega-banks.

Henrich, Joseph. *The Secret of Our Success: How Culture Is Driving Human Evolution, Domesticating Our Species, and Making Us Smarter.* Princeton: Princeton University Press, 2016.

Hill, Linda, and Kent Lineback. *Being the Boss: The 3 Imperatives for Becoming a Great Leader.* Boston: Harvard Business School Publishing, 2011.

IBM. "Working Beyond Borders: Insights from the Global Chief Human Resource Officer Study." *IBM Global Business Service,* September 2010.

Kahnweiler, Jennifer. *Quiet Influence: The Introvert's Guide to Making a Difference.* San Francisco: Berrett-Kohler Publishers, 2013.

Kaufman, Lindsey. "Google got it wrong. The open-office trend is destroying the workplace." *The Washington Post,* December 30, 2014. https://www.washingtonpost.com/posteverything/wp/2014/12/30/google-got-it-wrong-the-open-office-trend-is-destroying-the-workplace.

Kotter, John P. "Hierarch and Network: Two Structures, One Organization." *Harvard Business Review Blogs,* May 23, 2011. https://hbr.org/2011/05/two-structures-one-organizatio or http://bit.ly/1mvrywi.

——. "What Leaders Really Do." *Harvard Business Review,* December 2001. https://hbr.org/2001/12/what-leaders-really-do/ar/1 or http://bit.ly/1PlQQaj.

Kwiecinski, Tomek. "18 Reasons to Go to a Coach or Therapist." Imprific.com, January 8, 2016. https://imprific.com/tomkwiecinski/18-reasons-to-go-to-coach-or-therapist/.

Lencioni, Patrick M. *The Five Dysfunctions of a Team: A Leadership Fable.* San Francisco: John Wiley and Sons, 2002.

Melvill, Henry. *The Golden Lectures.* London: James Paul, 1855.

Monbiot, George. *Out of the Wreckage: A New Politics for an Age of Crisis.* London: Verso Books, 2107. Kindle Edition.

O'Conner, Patricia T., and Stewart Kellerman. "Extrovert or extravert?" *The Grammarphobia Blog,* January 11, 2016. https://www.grammarphobia.com/blog/2016/01/extrovert-extravert.html.

Pfeffer, Jeffrey. *Power: Why Some People Have It—and Others Don't.* New York: Harper Collins, 2010. Kindle Edition.

Pink, Daniel H. *Drive: The Surprising Truth About What Motivates Us.* New York: Riverhead Books, 2009.

Prevost, Larry. "Quick and Easy Way to Remembering Names." *Dale Carnegie Training.* http://www.dcarnegietraining.com/resources/remembering-names.

Robson, David. "Why We Should Celebrate Shyness." *BBC Future,* August 31, 2016. http://www.bbc.com/future/story/20160830-why-we-should-celebrate-shyness.

Schoenberger, Chana R. "How Performance Reviews Can Harm Mental Health." *The Wall Street Journal,* October 26, 2015. https://www.wsj.com/articles/how-performance-reviews-can-harm-mental-health-1445824925.

Schwartz, Tony, and Jim Loehr. *The Power of Full Engagement: Managing Energy, Not Time, Is the Key to High Performance and Personal Renewal.* New York: Simon & Schuster, 2003.

Schweer, Margaret, Dimitris Assimakopoulos, Rob Cross, and Robert J. Thomas. "Building a Well-Networked Organization." *MIT Sloan Management Review,* Winter 2012.

Stout, Martha. *The Sociopath Next Door: The Ruthless Versus the Rest of Us.* New York: Broadway Books, 2005.

Trevor, Jonathon, and Barry Varcoe. "How Aligned Is Your Organization?" *Harvard Business Review*, February 2017. https://hbr.org/2017/02/how-aligned-is-your-organization.

Weisenthal, Joe. "We Love What Warren Buffett Says About Life, Luck, And Winning The 'Ovarian Lottery.'" *Business Insider,* December 10, 2013. http://www.businessinsider.com/warren-buffett-on-the-ovarian-lottery-2013-12.

Welch, Jack. *Jack: Straight from the Gut.* New York: Hachette Book Group, 2003.